Communications in Computer and Information Science 2210

Series Editors

Gang Li ⓘ, *School of Information Technology, Deakin University, Burwood, VIC, Australia*
Joaquim Filipe ⓘ, *Polytechnic Institute of Setúbal, Setúbal, Portugal*
Ashish Ghosh ⓘ, *Indian Statistical Institute, Kolkata, West Bengal, India*
Zhiwei Xu, *Chinese Academy of Sciences, Beijing, China*

Rationale
The CCIS series is devoted to the publication of proceedings of computer science conferences. Its aim is to efficiently disseminate original research results in informatics in printed and electronic form. While the focus is on publication of peer-reviewed full papers presenting mature work, inclusion of reviewed short papers reporting on work in progress is welcome, too. Besides globally relevant meetings with internationally representative program committees guaranteeing a strict peer-reviewing and paper selection process, conferences run by societies or of high regional or national relevance are also considered for publication.

Topics
The topical scope of CCIS spans the entire spectrum of informatics ranging from foundational topics in the theory of computing to information and communications science and technology and a broad variety of interdisciplinary application fields.

Information for Volume Editors and Authors
Publication in CCIS is free of charge. No royalties are paid, however, we offer registered conference participants temporary free access to the online version of the conference proceedings on SpringerLink (http://link.springer.com) by means of an http referrer from the conference website and/or a number of complimentary printed copies, as specified in the official acceptance email of the event.

CCIS proceedings can be published in time for distribution at conferences or as post-proceedings, and delivered in the form of printed books and/or electronically as USBs and/or e-content licenses for accessing proceedings at SpringerLink. Furthermore, CCIS proceedings are included in the CCIS electronic book series hosted in the SpringerLink digital library at http://link.springer.com/bookseries/7899. Conferences publishing in CCIS are allowed to use Online Conference Service (OCS) for managing the whole proceedings lifecycle (from submission and reviewing to preparing for publication) free of charge.

Publication process
The language of publication is exclusively English. Authors publishing in CCIS have to sign the Springer CCIS copyright transfer form, however, they are free to use their material published in CCIS for substantially changed, more elaborate subsequent publications elsewhere. For the preparation of the camera-ready papers/files, authors have to strictly adhere to the Springer CCIS Authors' Instructions and are strongly encouraged to use the CCIS LaTeX style files or templates.

Abstracting/Indexing
CCIS is abstracted/indexed in DBLP, Google Scholar, EI-Compendex, Mathematical Reviews, SCImago, Scopus. CCIS volumes are also submitted for the inclusion in ISI Proceedings.

How to start
To start the evaluation of your proposal for inclusion in the CCIS series, please send an e-mail to ccis@springer.com.

Dong Hao · Bin Li · Swaprava Nath · Taiki Todo ·
Dengji Zhao
Editors

Mechanism Design in Social Networks

First International Workshop, MNet 2024
Held in Conjunction with IJCAI 2024
Jeju, South Korea, August 4, 2024
Proceedings

Editors
Dong Hao
University of Electronic Science
and Technology of China
Chengdu, China

Swaprava Nath
Indian Institute of Technology Bombay
Mumbai, Maharashtra, India

Dengji Zhao
ShanghaiTech University
Shanghai, China

Bin Li
Nanjing University of Science
and Technology
Nanjing, China

Taiki Todo
Kyushu University
Fukuoka, Japan

ISSN 1865-0929   ISSN 1865-0937 (electronic)
Communications in Computer and Information Science
ISBN 978-981-96-0213-1   ISBN 978-981-96-0214-8 (eBook)
https://doi.org/10.1007/978-981-96-0214-8

© The Editor(s) (if applicable) and The Author(s), under exclusive license
to Springer Nature Singapore Pte Ltd. 2025

This work is subject to copyright. All rights are solely and exclusively licensed by the Publisher, whether the whole or part of the material is concerned, specifically the rights of translation, reprinting, reuse of illustrations, recitation, broadcasting, reproduction on microfilms or in any other physical way, and transmission or information storage and retrieval, electronic adaptation, computer software, or by similar or dissimilar methodology now known or hereafter developed.
The use of general descriptive names, registered names, trademarks, service marks, etc. in this publication does not imply, even in the absence of a specific statement, that such names are exempt from the relevant protective laws and regulations and therefore free for general use.
The publisher, the authors and the editors are safe to assume that the advice and information in this book are believed to be true and accurate at the date of publication. Neither the publisher nor the authors or the editors give a warranty, expressed or implied, with respect to the material contained herein or for any errors or omissions that may have been made. The publisher remains neutral with regard to jurisdictional claims in published maps and institutional affiliations.

This Springer imprint is published by the registered company Springer Nature Singapore Pte Ltd.
The registered company address is: 152 Beach Road, #21-01/04 Gateway East, Singapore 189721, Singapore

If disposing of this product, please recycle the paper.

Preface

The tremendous development of the Internet has given rise to a variety of social networks and social-networking-driven markets. Understanding how social norms emerge from the interactions of distributed individuals and how to design institutions/markets to impact the outcomes of individuals' interactions is critical for reasoning about the highly connected world. The anonymity, complexity, and distributed nature of social networks complicate the way individuals interact with each other. Therefore, understanding or designing the incentives behind their behavior is very crucial to underpin the healthy development of social networks.

To facilitate the study of incentives on social networks, we organized The first International Workshop on Mechanism Design in Social Networks (MNet), a pivotal event that brought together leading researchers from AI agents, algorithmic game theory, and the social, economic, management, and organizational sciences. MNet 2024 was part of the IJCAI 2024 conference, which took place in Jeju, South Korea from 3rd to 9th of August, 2024.

The aim of the workshop was to provide an internationally respected forum for scientific research tackling the fundamental challenges of mechanism design in social networks. We received a total of 21 submissions, each reviewed by 2–3 reviewers. The review process was double-blind, and ultimately, 8 papers were accepted. As a representative interface integrating economics, game theory, and artificial intelligence, mechanism design takes both theoretical and engineering approaches to solve a wide range of problems involving interactions among individuals, markets, and institutions. Research on mechanism design has brought many novel solutions to practice, such as online advertisements, spectrum allocations, kidney exchanges, student-school matching systems, and digital economy platforms. However, traditional settings/solutions did not specifically touch the complexity of individuals' interactions in social networks. To combat this, since 2017, we have seen blooming studies focusing on mechanism design problems in social networks, including auctions, matching, cooperative games, and many other games in social networks. Almost all traditional games/mechanisms can be revisited within the network setting. Hence, we hope this workshop stimulated studies of this kind, and offered a platform to related researchers and practitioners to swiftly exchange mature and immature ideas.

We are very grateful for the contributors to the first edition of this workshop. We would also like to express our gratitude to Springer Nature for publishing the proceedings.

August 2024

Dong Hao
Bin Li
Swaprava Nath
Taiki Todo
Dengji Zhao

Organization

Organizing Committee

Dong Hao	University of Electronic Science and Technology of China, China
Bin Li	Nanjing University of Science and Technology, China
Swaprava Nath	Indian Institute of Technology Bombay, India
Taiki Todo	Kyushu University, Japan
Dengji Zhao	ShanghaiTech University, China

Program Committee

Ludwig Dierks	University of Illinois at Chicago, USA
Zhiyi Fan	University of Electronic Science and Technology of China, China
Yaoxin Ge	ShanghaiTech University, China
Yuhang Guo	University of New South Wales, Australia
Yifan Huang	University of Electronic Science and Technology of China, China
Bo Li	Hong Kong Polytechnic University, China
Haoxin Liu	ShanghaiTech University, China
Jiamou Liu	University of Auckland, New Zealand
Sangdan Luozhu	University of Electronic Science and Technology of China, China
Qi Shi	University of Southampton, UK
Xinwei Song	ShanghaiTech University, China
Shaozheng Zhang	University of Electronic Science and Technology of China, China
Yao Zhang	ShanghaiTech University, China
Yuxin Zhao	ShanghaiTech University, China
Yuyu Zhao	University of Electronic Science and Technology of China, China

Contents

Sybil-Proof Mechanism for Information Propagation with Budgets 1
   Junjie Zheng, Xu Ge, Bin Li, and Dengji Zhao

Comparison Between Public and Private Signals in Network Congestion
Games: Extended Abstract 19
   Akira Matsushita

Cascading Power 36
   Thomas Ågotnes and Zoé Christoff

Proposal of a Double Feedback Digital Product Ranking System 52
   Yuchen Liu, Rafik Hadfi, and Takayuki Ito

A Summary of Core-Competitiveness in Partially Observable Networked
Market 65
   Bin Li and Dong Hao

Incentives for Early Arrival in Cooperative Games: A Summary 76
   Yaoxin Ge, Yao Zhang, and Dengji Zhao

A Strategy-Proof and Collusion-Proof Peer Grading Mechanism 86
   Bin Li and Xiaoyu Du

A Summary of Distributed Mechanism Design in Social Networks 95
   Haoxin Liu and Yao Zhang

Author Index 111

Sybil-Proof Mechanism for Information Propagation with Budgets

Junjie Zheng[1], Xu Ge[1], Bin Li[2], and Dengji Zhao[1]([✉])

[1] ShanghaiTech University, Shanghai, China
{zhengjj,gexu,zhaodj}@shanghaitech.edu.cn
[2] Nanjing University of Science and Technology, Nanjing, China
cs.libin@njust.edu.cn

Abstract. This research investigates the problem of reward distribution in social networks to increase the effectiveness of crowdsourcing tasks for sponsors. Our goal is to design reward mechanisms that encourage early adopters to actively recruit more contributors, thereby streamlining task completion. However, participants may resort to strategic manoeuvres such as withholding invitations, exaggerating their task skills, or fabricating identities (Sybil attacks) to maximize personal gains. To address this dilemma, we introduce a novel mechanism, called the Propagation Reward Distribution Mechanism (PRDM), which effectively motivates agents to exert maximum effort, disseminate tasks throughout their social networks, and discourages Sybil attacks.

Keywords: Social Network · Reward Mechanism · Sybil Attack

1 Introduction

The widespread availability of mobile Internet devices has fostered greater interconnectedness among individuals via social networks and amplified the impact of information spread through social connections. In certain fields, including viral marketing [11], crowdsourcing distribution [6,17], answer querying [10], sponsors frequently incentivize participants with monetary rewards to gather as much data or sell as many products as possible. In 2005, Amazon launched a crowdsourcing platform called Amazon Mechanical Turk (MTurk) to gather data from non-professionals. On the MTurk platform, the sponsors can post tasks and rewards, and then the workers claim the tasks and receive payments accordingly based on the quantity and quality of their completed tasks. Many studies requiring extensive data started collecting data through MTurk [18]. One study in 2019 showed that more than 250,000 people have completed at least one task on MTurk [15]. However, a large percentage of these workers are fixed, which is mainly because that inviting new people to join is not beneficial. Making existing workers invite more people to participate can significantly improve efficiency.

© The Author(s), under exclusive license to Springer Nature Singapore Pte Ltd. 2025
D. Hao et al. (Eds.): MNET 2024, CCIS 2210, pp. 1–18, 2025.
https://doi.org/10.1007/978-981-96-0214-8_1

In this paper, we aim to adequately utilize people's connections in the network to design a reward distribution mechanism [26]. This mechanism incentivizes agents to invite more people to participate by the reward distribution, which eventually improves the overall completion efficiency. The first difficulty is distributing the rewards within a constrained budget. The mechanism should motivate agents to spread the information in their social network as much as possible. In the DARPA network challenge [14,19], the winning team from MIT used a pioneering mechanism to effectively motivate people to spread information and quickly found all ten red balloons. In multi-level marketing [7,8], the seller expects to sell more products by attracting more people to purchase. In our setting, we also need to properly allocate the limited budget to participants.

Another difficulty is resolving Sybil attacks in social networks. A Sybil attack is when participants create multiple false identities to accomplish specific purposes. Sybil attacks are widespread and easily performed, affecting eventual results and harming others [1,22,23]. Traditional defense approaches are mainly focused on the communication domain [5,24]. Scholars have extensively studied this phenomenon in various domains, such as the Vickrey-Clarke-Groves process in auction theory is vulnerable to Sybil attacks [21], and Yokoo et al. [20] developed a new protocol against false-name bids. In Bitcoin transactions, Babaioff et al. [2] devised a scheme that rewards information propagation to prevent Sybil attacks to make more revenue. In crowdsourcing, individuals have different abilities, such as computing power, purchasing advertising, or providing data. Emek et al. [9] solved the problem of Sybil attacks in viral marketing by rewarding propagation behavior based on the size of a maximum perfect binary tree. We aim to use this authentic contribution information to design an information propagation mechanism that defends against Sybil attacks.

In this paper, our mechanism drives improvements in the following dimensions.

- We propose a model that quantifies an agent's contribution by introducing the concept of capacity. The model considers the general setting of Sybil attacks.
- We propose a novel natural mechanism to allocate rewards that maximize information propagation within a limited budget while resisting Sybil attacks.

Related Work. With a fixed budget, Shi et al. [16] devised a mechanism that maximizes information propagation but is not resistant to Sybil attacks. Chen et al. [4] designed a special scenario of a free market with lotteries, where participants have a strong incentive to maximize the diffusion of information, and false-name manipulations fail to yield excessive rewards. In the answer querying problem, Zhang et al. [25] designed a mechanism that incentivizes the agents to propagate the requestor's query information while making the Sybil attack unavailable for additional gain. However, their mechanism only solves the scene of a single problem query in a tree. Hong et al. [3] solved the problem of Sybil attacks by removing possible fake agents by graph-structured methods, providing a new approach to tackle similar issues.

The remainder of this paper is organized as follows. Section 2 describes the fundamental setup and definition of the model. Section 3 shows our mechanism and an example of running the mechanism. Section 4 shows the properties of our mechanism. In Sect. 5, we discuss these properties. In Sect. 6, we summarize our work and discuss possible future directions.

2 The Model

We consider the crowdsourcing problem powered by social networks, where a sponsor expects to leverage the social connections to recruit more participants (or agents) to some crowdsourcing task, e.g., data collecting. For convenience, we model the social connections of all agents as a directed graph $G = (V, E)$, where V represents the set of vertices and E denotes the edge set. Except for the sponsor s, the graph G consists of a set $N = \{1, \ldots, n\}$ of agents who can contribute to the task, i.e., $V = \{s\} \cup N$. For each agent $i \in N$, we denote by c_i the maximum contribution capacity (or simply, capacity) of i for the task, e.g., c_i can denote the affordable number of pictures that need to be labeled. For any two agents $i, j \in V$, there is an edge $(i, j) \in E$ if and only if agent i can invite agent j. Given an edge $(i, j) \in E$, we say j is a child of i and use n_i to denote the set of i's children in G. Without promotions, the sponsor can only recruit her direct children n_s to the task, and within such small number of participants the task may fail to be accomplished. To attract more agents, the sponsor plans to reward the participants to incentivize them to further spread the task information to their children, under a total budget of B, and the amount of each participant's reward is determined by her reports, including her performance on the task and her diffusion efforts.

As usual, let $t_i = (n_i, c_i)$ be agent i's private type, where n_i denotes the set of her children and $c_i > 0$ is her capacity. In addition, denote by $\mathbf{t} = (t_1, \ldots, t_n)$ the type profile of all agents, and $\mathbf{t}_{-i}$ the type profile of all agents except agent i, i.e., $\mathbf{t} = (t_i, \mathbf{t}_{-i})$. For convenience's sake, we use $\mathcal{T}_i = \mathcal{P}(N) \times \mathbb{R}^+$ to denote the type space of agent i where $\mathcal{P}(N)$ is the power set of the set N, and $\mathcal{T} = \times \mathcal{T}_i$ to denote the space of all type profiles. As t_i is private information, agent i can cheat the sponsor to benefit herself. Let $t'_i = (n'_i, c'_i)$ be the type reported by agent i, i.e., i diffused information to n'_i and contributed c'_i to the task. Since agent i is unaware of other agents in the graph who are not her children and cannot contribute more than her capacity, we require that $n'_i \subseteq n_i$ and $c'_i \in (0, c_i]$. Similarly, let $\mathbf{t}' = (t'_i, \mathbf{t}'_{-i})$ denote the report profile of all agents, where $\mathbf{t}'_{-i}$ represents the report profile of all agents except agent i. Accordingly, we use $\mathcal{T}'_i = \mathcal{P}(n_i) \times (0, c_i]$ to denote the space of t'_i, $\mathcal{T}' = \times \mathcal{T}'_i$ the space of $\mathbf{t}'$, and $\mathcal{T}'_{-i} = \times_{j \neq i} \mathcal{T}'_j$ the space of $\mathbf{t}'_{-i}$.

Definition 1. *Given a report profile* $\mathbf{t}'$, *we say agent* i *is active if there exists an agent sequence* $\{i_1, i_2, \ldots, i_k\}$, *where* $i_1 \in n_s, i \in n'_{i_k}$ *and* $i_j \in n'_{i_{j-1}}$ *holds for* $1 < j \leq k$.

That is, an agent is an active agent if there is a "diffusion path" from the sponsor to her. Note that only active agents are real participants of the crowdsourcing task. Based on the definition of active agents, we next introduce the concept of active network.

Definition 2. *Given a report profile* $\mathbf{t}'$, *we use* $G(\mathbf{t}') = (V(\mathbf{t}'), E(\mathbf{t}'))$ *(or* $G' = (V', E')$ *for short) to denote the* **active network** *generated by* $\mathbf{t}'$, *where* V' *is the set of all active agents and* $E' = \{(i,j) | (i \in V', j \in n_i') \vee (i = s, j \in n_s)\}$.

The active network represents all agents that do participate in the task. Given any report profile $\mathbf{t}'$, the sponsor only need to reward agents in the active networks.

Definition 3. *A* **reward distribution mechanism** $M = (r_i)_{i \in N}$ *on the social network consists of a set of reward functions, where* $r_i : \mathcal{T}' \to \mathbb{R}$ *is the reward function for* i *and* $r_i(\mathbf{t}') = 0$ *for an inactive agent* i.

Given any report profile $\mathbf{t}' \in \mathcal{T}'$, $r_i(\mathbf{t}')$ outputs the reward to i. If an agent is not in the active network, her reward is always zero as she does not participate in the task and contributes nothing. When $\mathbf{t}'$ is clear from the context, we write as $\mathbf{r}$ and r_i for short. In the following, we define some desirable properties that a reward mechanism should satisfy. First, the reward mechanism should be individually rational, which guarantees that each participant is willing to stay in the mechanism.

Definition 4. *A reward distribution mechanism* M *is* **individually rational** *(IR) if* $r_i(\mathbf{t}') \geq 0$ *for all graph* G, *all* $i \in N$ *and all report profile* $\mathbf{t}' \in \mathcal{T}'$.

If a reward mechanism is not individually rational, then in certain cases some participants will pay to the sponsor and the best reply is leaving the mechanism. Therefore, the individually rational property is also known as the participation constraint. Besides the IR property, the sponsor also expects an agent to authentically contribute all her abilities and invite all her children to the task.

Definition 5. *A reward distribution mechanism* M *is* **incentive compatible** *(IC) if the following inequality*

$$r_i(t_i, \mathbf{t}'_{-i}) \geq r_i(t_i', \mathbf{t}'_{-i}) \tag{1}$$

holds for all graph G, *all* $i \in N$, *all* $t_i \in \mathcal{T}_i$, *all* $t_i' \in \mathcal{T}_i'$ *and all* $\mathbf{t}'_{-i} \in \mathcal{T}'_{-i}$.

Incentive compatibility implies that diffusing the task information to all children and contributing all her efforts to the task is a dominant strategy for all agents. As the sponsor is endowed with a fixed budget, the total rewards to agents are limited.

Definition 6. *A reward distribution mechanism* M *is* **budget balanced** *(BB) if*

$$\sum_{i=1}^{n} r_i(\mathbf{t}') = B \tag{2}$$

for all graph G, *all* $i \in N$ *and all report profile* $\mathbf{t}' \in \mathcal{T}'$.

Definition 7. *A reward distribution mechanism M is **asymptotically budget balanced** (ABB) if*

$$\lim_{\sum_{i \in N} c'_i \to \infty} \sum_{i \in N} r_i(\mathbf{t'}) = B \qquad (3)$$

for all graph G, all $i \in N$ and all report profile $\mathbf{t'} \in \mathcal{T'}$.

The ABB property requires the sponsor's budget to be fully distributed to agents when the sum of all agents' contributions goes to infinity. If a reward mechanism is IR and IC, then agents are motivated to contribute all their capacities and propagate the task information to all their children. However, as the agents are individuals distributed in the network, they can easily create fake identities or even fake social networks to gain more reward. Such behaviors are called Sybil attack or false-name attack, and a good reward mechanism should prevent such kind of behavior.

Definition 8. *A **Sybil attack** of agent i is denoted by an attacking type report $a_i = (\nu_i, \tau_i) \in \mathcal{A}_i$, where $\nu_i = \{i, i_1, \ldots, i_m\}$ is a set of fake identities and accordingly $\tau_i = \{t'_i, t'_{i_1}, \ldots, t'_{i_m}\}$ are their reports, where*

- $\sum_{j \in \nu_i} c'_j \leq c_i$;
- $n'_j \subseteq n_i \cup \nu_i$ for all $j \in \nu_i$.

In other words, agent i can create arbitrary number of fake identities and arbitrary social connections between these identities. Let us consider a special case of Sybil attack: all the fake nodes are invited by the inviters of node i.

Definition 9. *A **parallel Sybil attack** of agent i is a special kind of Sybil attack, where $\nu_i = \{i, i_1, \ldots, i_m\}$ is a set of fake identities invited by the parents of i.*

A Parallel Sybil attack implies only fake in parallel, where the fake participants are all invited by at least one inviter of the agent committing the attack.

Definition 10. *A reward distribution mechanism is **Sybil-proof** (SP), if the inequality*

$$\sum_{j \in \nu_i} r_j(a_i, \mathbf{t'}_{-i}) \leq r_i(t_i, \mathbf{t'}_{-i}) \qquad (4)$$

*holds for all graph G, all $i \in N$, all $t_i \in \mathcal{T}_i$, all $\mathbf{t'}_{-i} \in \mathcal{T'}_{-i}$ and $a_i \in \mathcal{A}_i$, where $(a_i, \mathbf{t'}_{-i}) = (t'_i, t'_{i_1}, \ldots, t'_{i_m}, \mathbf{t'}_{-i})$ is the report profile of all agents under Sybil attack a_i. The mechanism is **parallel Sybil-proof** (PSP) if the Sybil attacks satisfy the situation of parallel Sybil attacks.*

The SP property may be too strong to be held, and we next introduce a mild condition for Sybil-proofness, called γ-SP.

Definition 11. *A reward distribution mechanism is **γ-Sybil-proof** (γ-SP), if the inequality*

$$\sum_{j \in \nu_i} r_j(a_i, \mathbf{t'}_{-i}) \leq \gamma r_i(t_i, \mathbf{t'}_{-i}) \qquad (5)$$

holds for all graph $G = (V, E)$, all $i \in N$, all $t_i \in \mathcal{T}_i$, all $\mathbf{t'}_{-i} \in \mathcal{T'}_{-i}$ and $a_i \in \mathcal{A}_i$.

In the following contents, we focus on designing reward mechanisms that satisfy IR, IC and other expected properties.

3 Propagation Reward Distribution Mechanism

This section introduces a novel reward distribution mechanism called *Propagation Reward Distribution Mechanism* (PRDM). PRDM starts by layering a given network and then determines the final rewards for each agent by the contribution phase and propagation phase.

The goal of all agents is to get more rewards except that the sponsor wants to maximize the information propagation instead of receiving a reward. Sponsor s will always diffuse the information to all the children. For a given report profile $\mathbf{t}'$, we generate the active network $G(\mathbf{t}') = (V(\mathbf{t}'), E(\mathbf{t}'))$. In G', define the depth of agent i as the length of the shortest path from s to i, written as $dep(i)$. Therefore, different agents can be divided into different layers based on their depths, and define the k-th layer $l_k = \{i \in V' | dep(i) = k\}$ as the set of all agents with depth k.

Since we only allow information to be propagated from the previous layer to the next layer, for all $i \in l_k$, only the edges from agent i to the agents in the $(k+1)$-th layer are retained. By the above processing, we construct a layered directed graph based on $\mathbf{t}'$. Figure 1 shows an example of how to get the corresponding layered graph from an active network. In the obtained layered graph, for any $i \in l_k$, define p_i as the set of all parents of i in $(k-1)$-th layer.

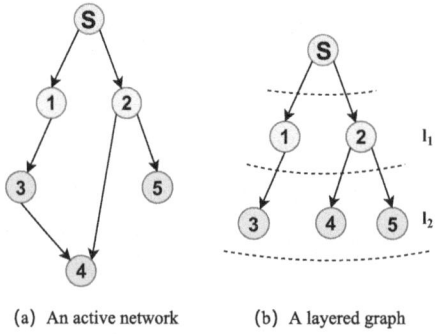

(a) An active network   (b) A layered graph

Fig. 1. An example of transforming an active network (a) into a layered graph (b).

PRDM is divided into a *contribution phase* and a *propagation phase*. In the contribution phase, the corresponding weight is determined by each agent's depth and contribution. In the propagation phase, the weight is redistributed according to agents' propagation and output agents' final reward. In PRDM, the parameter c_s is a virtual capacity of the sponsor, which is utilized to deliver the budget to the following layers. The parameter β measures what proportion of the rewards an agent gives her invitees. With the above definitions, the general procedure of PRDM is shown in Algorithm 1.

Algorithm 1: Propagation Reward Distribution Mechanism

Input: A report profile $\mathbf{t}'$, a fixed budget B and parameters $c_s > 0$ and $\beta \in [0, 1/2]$

1. Construct the active network $G(\mathbf{t}') = (V(\mathbf{t}'), E(\mathbf{t}'))$;
2. Compute the depth of each agent who is on the graph $G(\mathbf{t}')$ to obtain the layer sets $l_1, l_2, \ldots, l_d$;
3. For $k = 1, 2, \ldots, d$, let $C'_k = c_s + \sum_{i \in V(\mathbf{t}'), dep(i) \leq k} c'_i$ be the total contribution of s and layer $l_1, l_2, \ldots, l_k$;
4. **Contribution phase**: Initialize each agent's weight $w_i = 0$ for $i \in N$, and the initial budget of the first layer is $B_1 = B$;
5. **for** $k = 1, 2, \ldots, d$ **do**
6.   **for** each agent $i \in l_k$ **do**
7. $w_i = \frac{c'_i}{C'_k} B_k$;
8. $B_{k+1} = B_k - \sum_{i \in l_k} w_i$;
9. **Propagation phase**: Initialize each agent's reward $r_i = w_i$ for all $i \in l_1$, and $r_i = (1 - \beta) w_i$ for $i \in N \setminus l_1$;
10. **for** $k = 2, 3, \ldots, d$ **do**
11.   **for** each agent $i \in l_k$ **do**
12.   **for** each agent $j \in p_i$ **do**
13. $r_j = r_j + \frac{c'_j}{\sum_{m \in p_i} c'_m} \beta w_i$;

Output: the reward vector $\mathbf{r}(\mathbf{t}')$

3.1 An Example of PRDM

In this subsection, we show an example of the mechanism in operation. An instance is shown in Fig. 2 to give an illustration of PRDM. The sponsor transmits the information to the first layer $l_1 = \{1, 2, 3\}$. After that, $l_2 = \{4, 5, 6\}$ and $l_3 = \{7, 8\}$. The invitation relationships among all the agents are presented in Fig. 2(a).

Assuming a budget $B = 100$, we set $\beta = 0.2$ and $c_s = 20$, all agents report a contribution of 10. The process of distributing rewards using PRDM is as follows.

Contribution Phase:

- **Step 1:** C'_1 is the total contribution of sponsor s and agents 1, 2, and 3. We can calculate $C'_1 = 20 + 3 * 10 = 50$ and the budget $B_1 = B = 100$, so that each of them has weight

$$w_1 = w_2 = w_3 = \frac{10}{50} * 100 = 20$$

- **Step 2:** Calculate the budget $B_2 = B_1 - w_1 - w_2 - w_3 = 40$ and $C'_2 = C'_1 + 3 * 10 = 80$. Then we obtain the weight of the agent 4, 5, and 6 as

$$w_4 = w_5 = w_6 = \frac{10}{80} * 40 = 5$$

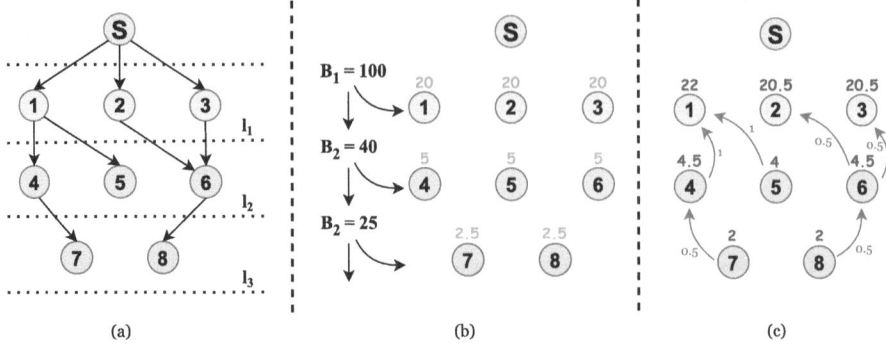

Fig. 2. An example of PRDM on input $B = 100$, $c_s = 20$, $\beta = 0.2$, each agent has a contribution of 10. (a) the invitation relationship among the sponsor and each agent. (b) each layer's initial budget B_k and each agent's weight w_i in contribution phase. (c) the transfer of reward during propagation phase and each agent's final reward r_i.

- **Step 3:** Similarly, $B_3 = B_2 - w_4 - w_5 - w_6 = 25$, $C_3' = C_2' + 2 * 10 = 100$, so the weight of agents 7 and 8 is

$$w_7 = w_8 = \frac{10}{100} * 25 = 2.5$$

Propagation Phase:

- **Step 4:** The initial reward for agents is the weight calculated in the contribution phase

$$r_1 = r_2 = r_3 = 20;$$
$$= r_5 = r_6 = (1 - \beta) * 5 = 4;$$
$$= r_8 = (1 - \beta) * 2.5 = 2$$

- **Step 5:** Agent 4 and agent 5 transfer 0.2 of their weights to agent 1 respectively as rewards; agent 6 transfers $\frac{\beta}{2} = \frac{0.2}{2} = 0.1$ of her weights to agent 2 and agent 3

$$\dashrightarrow r_1 = r_1 + \beta * w_4 = 21;$$
$$r_1 = r_1 + \beta * w_5 = 22;$$
$$r_2 = r_2 + \beta/2 * w_6 = 20.5,$$
$$r_3 = r_3 + \beta/2 * w_6 = 20.5$$

- **Step 6:** Similarly, we consider the transfer of agent 7 and agent 8

$$\dashrightarrow r_4 = r_4 + \beta * w_7 = 4.5;$$
$$r_6 = r_6 + \beta * w_8 = 4.5$$

The final reward is $\mathbf{r} = (22, 20.5, 20.5, 4.5, 4, 4.5, 2, 2)$ according to PRDM. Each component of $\mathbf{r}$ represents the reward of the corresponding agent. Note that we still have $B_4 = B_3 - w_7 - w_8 = 20$ available for further propagation.

4 Properties of PRDM

In this section, we show several properties of PRDM. We start by discussing the straightforward properties of PRDM, and then we illustrate how PRDM maximizes information propagation and defends against Sybil attacks.

For the convenience contents of the following formulation, denote C'_S as the sum of the contributions of the set S, e.g., C'_{l_k} is the total contribution of k-th layer. Recall that when k is an integer, C'_k denotes the total contribution of the first k layers.

Theorem 1. *The Propagation Reward Distribution Mechanism is asymptotically budget balanced.*

Proof. In PRDM, the division of the initial budget B is performed only in the contribution phase, which implies $\sum_{i \in N} r_i = \sum_{i \in N} w_i$. Recall that for an active network $G' = (V', E')$, the sponsor s has a virtual contribution $c_s > 0$ and $C'_k = c_s + \sum_{i \in V(\mathbf{t}'), dep(i) \leq k} c'_i$ is the total contribution of s and all the agents in layer $l_1, \ldots, l_k$.

According to PRDM, each layer can only divide a part of the remaining reward from the previous layer. Suppose that there are d layers. We focus on B_k, which is the residual budget of layer l_k inherited from the upper layer. Generally, for $k = 1, \ldots, d-1$, we have $B_{k+1} = B_k - \sum_{i \in l_k} w_i$. Specially, let $B_{d+1} = B_d - \sum_{i \in l_d} w_i$ be the budget that has not been distributed. Then, we can infer that

$$\sum_{i=1}^{n} r_i = \sum_{i=1}^{n} w_i = \sum_{k=1}^{d} \sum_{i \in l_k} w_i$$

$$= \sum_{k=1}^{d} (B_k - B_{k+1}) = B - B_{d+1}$$

Next, we show that B_{d+1} converges to 0 when the total contribution goes to infinity. Starting from the first layer, we can get

$$B_1 = B$$

$$B_2 = B_1 - \sum_{i \in l_1} w_i = B_1 - \sum_{i \in l_1} \frac{c'_i}{C'_1} B_1 = \frac{c_s}{C'_1} B$$

$$B_3 = B_2 - \sum_{i \in l_2} w_i = B_2 - \sum_{i \in l_2} \frac{c'_i}{C'_2} B_2 = \frac{c_s}{C'_2} B$$

Similarly, for $k = 2, \ldots, d$, we have $B_k = \frac{c_s}{C'_{k-1}} B$. Then, when the total contribution goes to infinity, $C'_d = \sum_{i=1}^{n} c'_i \to \infty$, hence $B_{d+1} = \frac{c_s}{C'_d} B \to 0$.

The above theorem indicates that PRDM will allocate all of the sponsor's budget to the agents when the total contribution is large enough. Meanwhile, the sponsor does not need to pay extra budgets for the contributions of extra participants.

Theorem 2. *The Propagation Reward Distribution Mechanism is individually rational.*

Proof. Intuitively, any agent i in a social network G, at any stage of PRDM, does not need to pay a fee, so $r_i \geq 0$ holds.

Actually, for any agent $i \in G(\mathbf{t}')$ of the active network, they always have a positive reward $r_i > 0$. Furthermore, Theorem 3 shows that an agent maximize the reward when she truthfully report her type.

Theorem 3. *The Propagation Reward Distribution Mechanism is incentive compatible.*

Proof. By the definition of incentive compatible, PRDM needs to satisfy that for any agent $i \in N$, for any report profile $\mathbf{t}'_{-i}$ of others, truthfully reporting her private type t_i is a dominant strategy. The report t'_i of agent i consists of the contributions c'_i and the set of children n'_i. Hence for any agent $i \in N$, we need to prove the following two parts

- Agent i contributes as much as she is capable $c'_i = c_i$ to maximize her reward.
- Agent i invites all her children $n'_i = n_i$ to maximize her reward.

Part 1: if agent i is not in the active network $G(\mathbf{t}') = (V(\mathbf{t}'), E(\mathbf{t}'))$, the reward is zero regardless of how much she contributes, so $c'_i = c_i$ maximizes her reward. For any $i \in V(\mathbf{t}')$, assume that agent i is in the k-th layer ($1 < k < d$) in the layered graph with d layers and agent i is the only parent of her children in $(k+1)$-th layer. Thus for any $0 < c'_i \leq c_i$, any $n'_i \subseteq n_i$ and $0 \leq \beta \leq \frac{1}{2}$, we have

$$r_i(t'_i, \mathbf{t}'_{-i}) = (1-\beta)\frac{c'_i}{C'_{k-1} + c'_i + C'_{l_k\setminus\{i\}}}B_k \\ + \beta\frac{C'_{l_{k+1}\cap n'_i}}{C'_{k-1} + c'_i + C'_{l_k\setminus\{i\}} + C'_{l_{k+1}}}\frac{C'_{k-1}}{C'_{k-1} + c'_i + C'_{l_k\setminus\{i\}}}B_k \quad (6)$$

where $C'_{l_k\setminus\{i\}}$ is the total contribution in k-th layer except i, $C_{l_{k+1}\cap n'_i}$ is the total contribution of i's children in $(k+1)$-th layer. The first term of $r_i(t'_i, \mathbf{t}'_{-i})$ in Eq. (6) is the reward reserved by i. The second term is the reward coming from the next layer. All quantities except c'_i are fixed, so the first term increases as c'_i increases and the second term decreases as c'_i increases. Consider the worst case: $C'_{l_k\setminus\{i\}} = 0$, $C_{l_{k+1}\cap n'_i} = C_{l_{k+1}}$, $\beta = \frac{1}{2}$ when the first term decreases the fastest while the second term increases the slowest, $r_i(t'_i, \mathbf{t}'_{-i})$ can be reduced as

$$r_i(t'_i, \mathbf{t}'_{-i})$$
$$= \frac{1}{2}\frac{1}{C'_{k-1}}\left(c'_i + \frac{C'_{k-1}C'_{l_{k+1}}}{C'_{k-1} + c'_i + C'_{l_{k+1}}}\right)B_k$$
$$= \frac{1}{2}\frac{1}{C'_{k-1}+c'_i}\frac{c'_iC'_{k-1} + c'_ic'_i + c'_iC'_{l_{k+1}} + C'_{k-1}C'_{l_{k+1}}}{C'_{k-1} + c'_i + C'_{l_{k+1}}}B_k$$
$$= \frac{1}{2}\frac{(C'_{k-1}+c'_i)(c'_i + C'_{l_{k+1}})}{(C'_{k-1}+c'_i)(C'_{k-1}+c'_i+C'_{l_{k+1}})}B_k$$
$$= \frac{1}{2}\frac{c'_i + C'_{l_{k+1}}}{C'_{k-1} + c'_i + C'_{l_{k+1}}}B_k \qquad (7)$$

Since $r_i(t'_i, \mathbf{t}'_{-i})$ is a monotonically increasing function of c'_i, agent i receives the highest reward when $c'_i = c_i$. Furthermore, if $k = 1$, agent i is in the first layer and is not required to distribute rewards to the previous layer, the first term in Eq. (6) will be larger. If $k = d$, agent i is in the last layer and has no rewards from the next layer, so the second term in Eq. (6) is 0. If agent i is not the only parent of her children in $(k+1)$-th layer, the second term in the Eq. (6) decreases more slowly. All of these cases will be better than the worst case we discussed in Eq. (7). Therefore $c'_i = c_i$ maximizes the reward of agent i.

Part 2: if agent i is not in the active network $G(\mathbf{t}') = (V(\mathbf{t}'), E(\mathbf{t}'))$, again her reward is always equal to 0. If $i \in V(\mathbf{t}')$, for all $n'_i \subset n_i$, she add one more child $j \in n_i$ into n'_i. Suppose agent j is already in $V(\mathbf{t}')$. In that case, we consider that j is in the layer below i, i gets an additional reward without affecting the existing reward, and i's reward remains unchanged if j is in other layers. Alternatively j is a new agent in the active network, then j must be in the next layer of i, the reward of i changes from $(1-\beta)\frac{c'_i}{C'_k}B_k + \beta\frac{C'_{l_{k+1}\cap n'_i}}{C'_{k+1}}B_{k+1}$ to $(1-\beta)\frac{c'_i}{C'_k}B_k + \beta\frac{c'_j+C'_{l_{k+1}\cap n'_i}}{c'_j+C'_{k+1}}B_{k+1}$, which is obviously increased. Hence when agent i invites all her children, she maximizes the reward.

In conclusion, PRDM is incentive compatible, which indicates that truthful report is the dominant strategy for all agents. In other words, all agents will maximize information propagation while making the largest contributions within their capacity.

Next, we will discuss the property of Sybil-proofness.

Theorem 4. *The Propagation Reward Distribution Mechanism is parallel Sybil-proof.*

Proof. Suppose agent $i \in l_k$ ($1 \le k \le d$). When agent i does commit a parallel Sybil attack to be $\nu_i = \{i, i_1, \ldots, i_m\}$. It can be simply deduced from the proof of incentive compatible that for all nodes in the set ν_i, their dominant strategy is making the largest contributions within their capacity and invites all their children. However, their capacity is limited by $\sum_{j \in \nu_i} c'_j \leq c_i$, which means that truthful reports without creating fake nodes will maximize the benefit of agent i.

Then we discuss the more general situation of Sybil attacks. Before giving the main conclusion, we first present two lemmas. Lemma 1 concludes that an agent cannot increase her weight in contribution phase by making fake nodes.

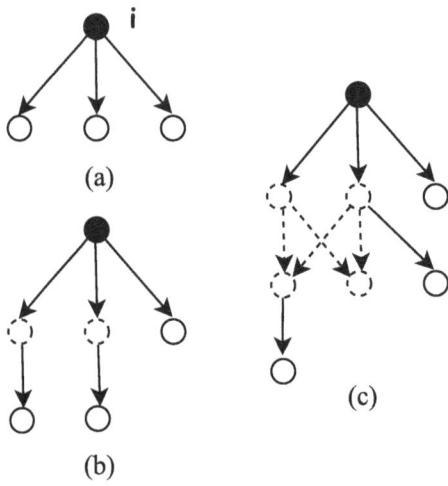

Fig. 3. (a) is the case where agent i does not commit Sybil attacks, the black node represents agent i, and the white nodes represent real participants that i invites. (b) shows the situation where i conducts fake nodes one layer down in which the dashed node represent all the nodes generated by i. (c) is the most general form of a Sybil attacks.

Lemma 1. *Each agent $i \in V(\mathbf{t}')$ cannot increase the total weight in contribution phase by committing Sybil attack $a_i = (\nu_i, \tau_i)$.*

Proof. Suppose agent $i \in l_k$ ($1 \leq k \leq d$). When agent i does not commit a Sybil attack, the network is shown in Fig. 3(a), the weight of i is $w_i = \frac{c'_i}{C'_k} B_k$. Let us first show that an agent cannot increase her weight by making several fake nodes as her own children. For convenience, we denote $\nu_{-i} = \nu_i \setminus \{i\}$.

Without loss of generality, let $c'_i = c_i$. After committing Sybil attack $a_i = (\nu_i, \tau_i)$, agent i can transfer part of her contribution δ to her fake nodes ($0 < \delta < c_i$) and $\sum_{j \in \nu_{-i}} c'_j = \delta$. Let $\mathcal{W}_i(\delta) = \sum_{j \in \nu_i} w_j$ be the total weight of i and all her fake nodes. According to PRDM, as shown in Fig. 3(b), when all the fake nodes are in the next layer of i, we have

$$\mathcal{W}_i(0) = \frac{c_i}{C'_{k-1} + c_i + C'_{l_k \setminus \{i\}}} B_k$$

$$\mathcal{W}_i(\delta) = \frac{c_i - \delta}{C'_{k-1} + c_i + C'_{l_k \setminus \{i\}} - \delta} B_k \tag{8}$$

$$+ \frac{\delta}{C'_{k-1} + c_i + C'_{l_k \setminus \{i\}} + C'_{l_{k+1} \setminus \nu_{-i}}} \frac{C'_{k-1}}{C'_{k-1} + c_i + C'_{l_k \setminus \{i\}} - \delta} B_k$$

It can be shown that for any δ, there is $\mathcal{W}_i(0) - \mathcal{W}_i(\delta) = \frac{P}{Q}$, where

$$P = \delta C'_{l_k \setminus \{i\}} \left(C'_{l_k \setminus \{i\}} + C'_{l_{k+1} \setminus \nu_{-i}} + C'_{k-1} + c_i \right)$$
$$+ \delta C'_{k-1} C'_{l_{k+1} \setminus \nu_{-i}} \geq 0$$

$$Q = \left(C'_{k-1} + c_i + C'_{l_k \setminus \{i\}} \right) \left(C'_{k-1} + c_i + C'_{l_k \setminus \{i\}} - \delta \right)$$
$$\left(C'_{k-1} + c_i + C'_{l_k \setminus \{i\}} + C'_{l_{k+1} \setminus \nu_{-i}} \right) > 0$$

Therefore, we have $\mathcal{W}_i(0) \geq \mathcal{W}_i(\delta)$, agent i cannot increase the total weight by committing Sybil attacks in Fig. 3(b). Let us consider the case $\mathcal{W}_i(0) = \mathcal{W}_i(\delta)$, which implies that $P = 0$. Then it can be obtained $C'_{l_k \setminus \{i\}} = 0$ and $C'_{l_{k+1} \setminus \nu_{-i}} = 0$, which shows that there are no other agents in the k-th and $k+1$-th layers. Recursively, the most general case in Fig. 3(c) can be generated by repeating the above steps. Therefore, we have $\mathcal{W}_i(0) \geq \mathcal{W}_i(\delta)$ for any Sybil attack a_i, agent i cannot increase her total weight by committing Sybil attacks.

The conclusion of the Lemma 2 is that an agent cannot make her reward from non-fake-node children (not i's fake nodes) too much by creating fake nodes. Here we give the majority assumption: $c_i \leq \left(\sqrt{\frac{1}{1-\beta}} - 1\right)\left(C'_{k-1} + C'_{l_k \setminus \{i\}}\right)$ which implies that agent i's capacity cannot take up $\left(\sqrt{\frac{1}{1-\beta}} - 1\right)$ times the sum of the capacity of i's layer and above which is similar to Bitcoin's 51% attack [13].

Lemma 2. *For $0 < \beta \leq \frac{1}{2}$, each agent $i \in V(\mathbf{t}')$ cannot increase $\frac{1}{1-\beta}$ times the reward received from her non-fake-node children by any Sybil attack $a_i = (\nu_i, \tau_i)$ under the majority assumption.*

Proof. Without loss of generality, let $c'_i = c_i$. After committing Sybil attack $a_i = (\nu_i, \tau_i)$, agent i can transfer part of her contribution δ to her fake nodes ($0 < \delta < c_i$). Let $\mathcal{R}_i(\delta)$ be the reward received from her non-fake-node children. If i does not commit a Sybil attack, the network is as shown in Fig. 3(a) and the reward is $\mathcal{R}_i(0)$. We have

$$\mathcal{R}_i(0) = \beta \frac{\sum_{j \in l_{k+1} \cap n'_i} \frac{c_i}{\sum_{m \in p_j} c'_m}}{C'_{k-1} + c_i + C'_{l_k \setminus \{i\}} + C'_{l_{k+1}}} \frac{C'_{k-1}}{C'_{k-1} + c_i + C'_{l_k \setminus \{i\}}} B_k$$

For a fixed δ, in Fig. 3(c), transferring more of δ to $(k+1)$-th layer of lower makes i receive more rewards from her non-fake-node children. Thus

$$\mathcal{R}_i(\delta) < \beta \frac{\sum_{j\in l_{k+1}\cap n'_i} \sum_{m\in p_j} \frac{c_i}{c'_m}}{C'_{k-1} + C'_{l_k\setminus\{i\}} + C'_{l_{k+1}}} \frac{C'_{k-1}}{C'_{k-1} + C'_{l_k\setminus\{i\}}} B_k$$

If $c_i \leq \left(\sqrt{\frac{1}{1-\beta}} - 1\right)\left(C'_{k-1} + C'_{l_k\setminus\{i\}}\right)$, which is the majority assumption, then

$$\frac{\mathcal{R}_i(\delta)}{\mathcal{R}_i(0)} < \frac{\left(C'_{k-1} + c_i + C'_{l_k\setminus\{i\}} + C'_{l_{k+1}}\right)\left(C'_{k-1} + c_i + C'_{l_k\setminus\{i\}}\right)}{\left(C'_{k-1} + C'_{l_k\setminus\{i\}} + C'_{l_{k+1}}\right)\left(C'_{k-1} + C'_{l_k\setminus\{i\}}\right)}$$

$$\leq \frac{\left(C'_{k-1} + c_i + C'_{l_k\setminus\{i\}}\right)^2}{\left(C'_{k-1} + C'_{l_k\setminus\{i\}}\right)^2} \leq \frac{1}{1-\beta}$$

Theorem 5. *The Propagation Reward Distribution Mechanism is $\frac{1}{1-\beta}$-Sybil-proof with $0 < \beta \leq \frac{1}{2}$ under the majority assumption.*

Proof. For an agent not in the active network, her reward is always 0, and Theorem 5 holds. For any agent $i \in V(\mathbf{t}')$, the reward of i has two parts, the first part comes from her weight, and the second part comes from her non-fake-node children. For all $t_i \in \mathcal{T}_i$, all $\mathbf{t}'_{-i} \in \mathcal{T}'_{-i}$ and $a_i \in \mathcal{A}_i$, combine Lemma 1 and Lemma 2, we have

$$\sum_{j\in\nu_i} r_j(a_i, \mathbf{t}'_{-i}) < \mathcal{W}_i(\delta) + \mathcal{R}_i(\delta)$$

$$\leq \frac{1}{1-\beta}(1-\beta)\mathcal{W}_i(0) + \frac{1}{1-\beta}\mathcal{R}_i(0)$$

$$\leq \frac{1}{1-\beta} r_i(t_i, \mathbf{t}'_{-i})$$

When $\beta = 0$, there is no reward for propagating information in this situation, and the mechanism is SP. When $\beta = \frac{1}{2}$, PRDM is 2-SP, which indicates an agent who commits any Sybil attack will not receive twice the reward she truthfully reports.

4.1 Example

Then we give an example to illustrate the incentive compatibility and Sybil-proofness below.

Example 1. The original active network is the same as Figure in paper. Consider the following two strategies that agent 1 may adopt respectively:

1. Agent 1 creates a fake node 9 as her children, and transfers δ of her contribution to 9.

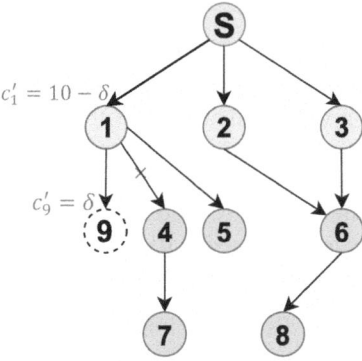

Fig. 4. The strategies agent 1 may adopt: agent 1 can transfer δ ($0 < \delta < 10$) of her contribution to agent 9 and she can disinvite agent 4.

2. Agent 1 does not invite agent 4.

The active network under agent 1's manipulation is shown in Fig. 4. In this case, agent 1's utility is the total reward of agent 1 and agent 9. The relationship between her utility and δ is shown in Fig. 5. From this figure, we can obtain the following conclusions.

1. Creating fake node 9 reduces agent i's utility.
2. Agent 1's utility decreases when she does not invite agent 4.

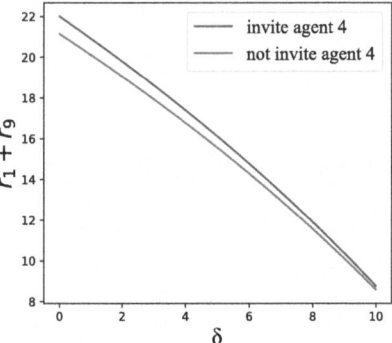

Fig. 5. Relationship between agent 1's total utility ($r_1 + r_9$) when agent 1 transfers δ of her contribution to her fake nodes ($0 < \delta < 10$), under both conditions whether she invites agent 4.

5 Discussion

Intuitively, there are somewhat conflicts between IC and SP. To satisfy incentive compatibility, we should give an extra reward to those agents who invite more participants. On the other hand, we should reduce the reward of agents who make fake identities to satisfy Sybil-proofness. In the scenario where capacity is not introduced, we define strong IC and strong SP as invitations that necessarily increase agent's reward and falsifications that necessarily decrease agent's reward. The following is an impossibility result.

Proposition 1. *If a reward distribution mechanism M satisfies both IC and SP, then it must be neither strong IC nor strong SP.*

Proof. In mechanism M, for any agent i, assume that the original reward is r_i^1 and the reward for inviting one more person j is r_i^2. Since it is impossible to distinguish whether the invited extra person is fake, IC requires $r_i^1 \leq r_i^2$ and SP requires $r_i^1 \geq r_i^2 + r_j$. Clearly we can obtain $r_j = 0$ and $r_i^1 = r_i^2$, which suggests that the mechanism M must be neither strong IC nor strong SP.

If we consider benevolent agent model in which each agent forwards the sale information even though such action does not bring her a higher utility, then the following trivial mechanism is IC and SP.

Mechanism 1. *Each agent $i \in n_s$ gets a reward of $B/|n_s|$ and other agents have no reward, where $|n_s|$ denotes the number of the sponsor's children.*

Obviously, the above mechanism satisfies IC and SP, but provides no incentive for agents to propagate the sale information. Studying SP mechanisms with strong diffusion incentives opens several avenues for the problem under investigation, which we leave for future work.

6 Conclusions

In this paper, we design a novel reward distribution mechanism for information propagation in social networks with limited budgets called Propagation Reward Distribution Mechanism. PRDM can achieve maximum information propagation and motivate all participants to contribute their maximum capacities while resisting Sybil attacks. PRDM is also asymptotically budget balanced.

At the same time, in addition to creating fake nodes alone, agents can collude (multiple individuals cooperating in manipulation) [12]. There is a trade-off among the aspects of Sybil attacks, collusion problem and incentive effect. Requiring all these properties leaves us with very limited design space. It is also an interesting topic to consider the trade-offs between these limitations.

Acknowledgement. This work is supported by Science and Technology Commission of Shanghai Municipality (No. 22ZR1442200 and No. 23010503000), Shanghai Frontiers Science Center of Human-centered Artificial Intelligence (ShangHAI), and National Natural Science Foundation of China (No. 62202229).

Disclosure of Interests. The authors have no competing interests to declare that are relevant to the content of this article.

References

1. Alothali, E., Zaki, N., Mohamed, E.A., Ashwal, H.A.: Detecting social bots on twitter: a literature review. In: 2018 International Conference on Innovations in Information Technology (IIT), Al Ain, United Arab Emirates, 18–19 November 2018, pp. 175–180. IEEE (2018)
2. Babaioff, M., Dobzinski, S., Oren, S., Zohar, A.: On bitcoin and red balloons. In: Proceedings of the 13th ACM Conference on Electronic Commerce, pp. 56–73 (2012),
3. Chen, H., Deng, X., Wang, Y., Wu, Y., Zhao, D.: Sybil-proof diffusion auction in social networks. CoRR abs/2211.01984 (2022)
4. Chen, J., Li, B.: Maximal information propagation via lotteries. In: Feldman, M., Fu, H., Talgam-Cohen, I. (eds.) WINE 2021. LNCS, vol. 13112, pp. 486–503. Springer, Cham (2022). https://doi.org/10.1007/978-3-030-94676-0_27
5. Chen, S., Pang, Z., Wen, H., Yu, K., Zhang, T., Lu, Y.: Automated labeling and learning for physical layer authentication against clone node and sybil attacks in industrial wireless edge networks. IEEE Trans. Ind. Inform. **17**(3), 2041–2051 (2021)
6. Doan, A., Ramakrishnan, R., Halevy, A.Y.: Crowdsourcing systems on the worldwide web. Commun. ACM **54**(4), 86–96 (2011). https://doi.org/10.1145/1924421.1924442
7. Drucker, F., Fleischer, L.: Simpler sybil-proof mechanisms for multi-level marketing. In: Proceedings of the 13th ACM Conference on Electronic Commerce, pp. 441–458 (2012)
8. Emek, Y., Karidi, R., Tennenholtz, M., Zohar, A.: Mechanisms for multi-level marketing. In: Proceedings 12th ACM Conference on Electronic Commerce, pp. 209–218 (2011)
9. Emek, Y., Karidi, R., Tennenholtz, M., Zohar, A.: Mechanisms for multi-level marketing. In: Shoham, Y., Chen, Y., Roughgarden, T. (eds.) Proceedings 12th ACM Conference on Electronic Commerce (EC-2011), San Jose, CA, USA, 5–9 June 2011, pp. 209–218. ACM (2011)
10. Kleinberg, J., Raghavan, P.: Query incentive networks. In: Proceedings of the 46th Annual IEEE Symposium on Foundations of Computer Science, pp. 132–141 (2005). https://doi.org/10.1109/SFCS.2005.63
11. Leskovec, J., Adamic, L.A., Huberman, B.A.: The dynamics of viral marketing. In: Proceedings of the 7th ACM Conference on Electronic Commerce, pp. 228–237 (2006). https://doi.org/10.1145/1134707.1134732
12. Marshall, R.C., Marx, L.M.: Bidder collusion. J. Econ. Theory **133**(1), 374–402 (2007)
13. Nakamoto, S.: Bitcoin: a peer-to-peer electronic cash system. Decentral. Bus. Rev. 21260 (2008)
14. Pickard, G., et al.: Time-critical social mobilization. Science **334**(6055), 509–512 (2011). https://doi.org/10.1126/SCIENCE.1205869
15. Robinson, J., Rosenzweig, C., Moss, A.J., Litman, L.: Tapped out or barely tapped? recommendations for how to harness the vast and largely unused potential of the mechanical Turk participant pool. PLoS ONE **14**(12), e0226394 (2019)

16. Shi, H., Zhang, Y., Si, Z., Wang, L., Zhao, D.: Maximal information propagation with budgets. In: Proceedings of the 24th European Conference on Artificial Intelligence. Front. Artif. Intell. Appl. 325, pp. 211–218 (2020)
17. Singer, Y., Mittal, M.: Pricing tasks in online labor markets. In: Proceedings of the 11th AAAI Conference on Human Computation, pp. 55–60 (2011)
18. Sorokin, A., Forsyth, D.A.: Utility data annotation with amazon mechanical Turk. In: IEEE Conference on Computer Vision and Pattern Recognition, pp. 1–8 (2008)
19. Tang, J.C., Cebrian, M., Giacobe, N.A., Kim, H.W., Kim, T., Wickert, D.B.: Reflecting on the Darpa red balloon challenge. Commun. ACM **54**(4), 78–85 (2011). https://doi.org/10.1145/1924421.1924441
20. Yokoo, M., Sakurai, Y., Matsubara, S.: Robust combinatorial auction protocol against false-name bids. Artif. Intell. **130**(2), 167–181 (2001)
21. Yokoo, M., Sakurai, Y., Matsubara, S.: The effect of false-name bids in combinatorial auctions: new fraud in internet auctions. Games Econ. Behav. **46**(1), 174–188 (2004)
22. Yu, H., Kaminsky, M., Gibbons, P.B., Flaxman, A.: Sybilguard: defending against sybil attacks via social networks, pp. 267–278 (2006)
23. Zhang, K., Liang, X., Lu, R., Shen, X.: Sybil attacks and their defenses in the internet of things. IEEE Internet Things J. **1**(5), 372–383 (2014)
24. Zhang, S., Lee, J.: Double-spending with a sybil attack in the bitcoin decentralized network. IEEE Trans. Ind. Inform. **15**(10), 5715–5722 (2019)
25. Zhang, Y., Zhang, X., Zhao, D.: Sybil-proof answer querying mechanism. In: Proceedings of the Twenty-Ninth International Joint Conference on Artificial Intelligence, IJCAI 2020, pp. 422–428 (2020)
26. Zhang, Y., Zhao, D.: Incentives to invite others to form larger coalitions. In: Faliszewski, P., Mascardi, V., Pelachaud, C., Taylor, M.E. (eds.) 21st International Conference on Autonomous Agents and Multiagent Systems, AAMAS 2022, Auckland, New Zealand, 9–13 May 2022, pp. 1509–1517. IFAAMAS (2022)

Comparison Between Public and Private Signals in Network Congestion Games
Extended Abstract

Akira Matsushita

Kyoto University, Yoshida-honmachi, Sakyo-ku, Kyoto-shi, Kyoto, Japan
amatsushita@i.kyoto-u.ac.jp

Abstract. This paper addresses an information design problem in a non-atomic network congestion game, where agents seek to move from their origins to their destinations through the fastest path. The information designer, who observes the true state of the world, sends signals to the agents to minimize the expected total travel time (ETTT). We explore two types of signaling policies: *public policies* and *private i.i.d. policies*. A public policy provides the same signal to all agents, while private i.i.d. policies can assign different signals to each agent, drawn from the pre-committed distribution. While the best i.i.d. policy consistently archives the lower ETTT, the best public policy is much easier to compute, utilizing a convexification approach. When each cost function is a sum of (i) an affine function of its share and (ii) state-dependent terms, perfect disclosure of the true state proves optimal among all public policies, achieving ETTT at most 4/3 times that of the best private i.i.d. policy. Finally, we introduce a deep neural network model to approximate the optimal private i.i.d. policy.

Keywords: congestion games · selfish routing · information design · potential games · game theory

1 Introduction

Today, many car navigation systems, including Google Maps and Waze, offer route recommendation services based on real-time road conditions. These systems gather extensive data on traffic congestion, accidents, and lane regulations from both public sources and user inputs, enabling them to identify the most efficient routes among numerous candidates. Consequently, these service providers are able to accurately determine the current state of roads, which the drivers hardly know by themselves. This scenario aligns well with the information design framework [3,7] in which an information designer (a navigation system provider) can observe the true state of the world and send signals to uninformed agents (drivers), according to the pre-programmed policy.

Although traffic navigation can be a good real-world application of the information design framework, typical apps only provide common information on road conditions and offer identical recommendations to all users. However, if these platforms were to offer more sophisticated and private recommendations to drivers, it could potentially reduce the average travel time from origin to destination.

In this research, we study a static non-atomic congestion game on a directed graph, often referred to as selfish routing, a topic that has been widely studied in both economics and computer science [2,4,10,11]. On a network, a continuum of agents seeks to move from their origins to destinations through the minimum travel time routes.

The primary difference between typical congestion games and our model lies in the existence of uncertainty. In our model, the edge *cost functions*, which determine the time required to pass through, depend on the state of the world that is unobservable to the agents. While agents are aware that a state is drawn from a known prior distribution, they do not have access to its realized value. In this environment, the information designer, who can observe the realized state, sends signals to induce the agents to play a Bayes correlated equilibrium with a lower expected total travel time (ETTT).

The objectives of the agents and the designer look similar, but they do not necessarily coincide due to the negative externality of road use. Let's see this through Example 1.

Example 1. Consider a unit mass of agents $I = [0,1]$ moves from the node v_1 to v_2 via one of the two paths: P_1 and P_2, as depicted in Fig. 1. The cost functions are given by $c_1(s_1, \omega) = \omega$ and $c_2(s_2, \omega) = s_2$ where s_1, s_2 are the shares of P_1, P_2. The cost of the route P_1 only depends on an unobservable state, while that of P_2 only depends on its share. The state $\omega \in \{0,1\}$ is drawn from the uniform prior $\Pr(\omega = 0) = \Pr(\omega = 1) = 0.5$, that is common knowledge to the agents.

The socially optimal shares of agents that minimize ETTT are $(s_1, s_2) = (1,0)$ when $\omega = 0$ and $(0.5, 0.5)$ when $\omega = 1$. The minimum ETTT is then $0.5 \times 0 + 0.5 \times 0.5 = 0.25$.

However, the socially optimal shares above are not sustained in equilibrium. If the designer discloses the true state when $\omega = 1$, the agents try to switch from P_1 to P_2 since the cost of P_2 is smaller: $c_1(0.5, 1) = 1 > c_2(0.5, 1) = 0.5$.

Taking agents' strategic behavior into account, the designer cannot attain the socially optimal ETTT of 0.25. The optimal policy, under incentive compatibility (IC) constraints of agents, recommends (i) $\frac{2+\sqrt{2}}{4}$ agents to P_1 and $\frac{2-\sqrt{2}}{4}$ agents to P_2 when $\omega = 0$, and (ii) recommends $\frac{\sqrt{2}}{4}$ agents to P_1 and $\frac{4-\sqrt{2}}{4}$ agents to P_2 when $\omega = 1$. This policy achieves the optimal ETTT $\frac{3-\sqrt{2}}{4} \simeq 0.3964$. The derivation of this optimal policy is detailed in Sect. 4.

This paper focuses on two types of signaling policies: *public policies* and *private i.i.d. policies*. A public policy provides the same signal to all agents, while private i.i.d. policies[1] can assign different signals to each agent, randomly drawn from the pre-committed distribution.

---

[1] A private i.i.d. policy is a policy in which the designer commits to a function that inputs a state and outputs a *share of agents* receiving each signal, rather than directly

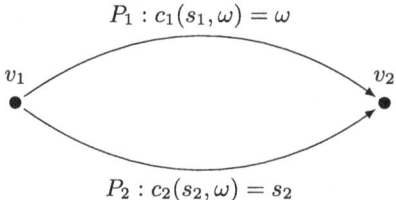

Fig. 1. A network and cost functions of Example 1. s_1, s_2 are the shares of agents who use P_1, P_2, respectively. $\omega \in \{0, 1\}$ is a realized state of the world that is unknown to agents.

Although some previous papers [5,8] analyze information design in congestion games, this paper contributes to the literature in the following points. First, we explicitly consider general networks rather than networks with only one origin and one destination. We demonstrate that the optimal public signaling policy can still be deduced by convexification of the expected total cost $C(\mu)$ given a common posterior among agents, μ, similar to [1,7].

Second, we found that if each cost function is of the form $c_e(s_e, \omega) = \alpha_e s_e + \kappa_e(\omega)$ for a constant $\alpha_e > 0$, which means each cost function is a sum of (i) an affine function of its share and (ii) a state-dependent cost, then the expected total cost function $C(\mu)$ given a common posterior μ becomes concave, which leads to the conclusion that the optimal public signaling policy is the perfect disclosure of true states. Then, it attains the ETTT at most $4/3$ times that of any policy, including the best private i.i.d. policy.

Finally, we analyzed the private i.i.d. policies. We formulated the optimization problem to compute the best i.i.d. policy, similar to that in [3]. However it turned out to be not a linear (in general) nor a convex problem. Despite the problem's difficulty, the best i.i.d. policy has proven to be always more efficient than the best public policy. Drawing inspiration from RegretNet as discussed in [6], we developed a deep learning model that approximates the optimal i.i.d. policy.

2 Model

2.1 Bayesian Congestion Game

Consider a directed network $N = (V, E)$ where $V = \{v_1, \ldots, v_m\}$ denotes a set of vertices and $E = \{e_1, \ldots, e_n\}$ a set of directed edges. On this network, a unit measure of agents $I = [0, 1]$ simultaneously moves from their origins to destinations. Let $f(v_i, v_j)$ (≥ 0) be a ratio of agents whose origin is v_i and destination is v_j. We assume $f(v, v) = 0$ for all $v \in V$ and $\sum_{v_i, v_j \in V^2} f(v_i, v_j) = 1$.

---

determines agents' signals to receive. Then, the signals for agents are randomly drawn from the distribution. In other words, a private i.i.d. policy means an *anonymous* policy. Although independence over infinite signals is not a mathematically well-defined concept, following the precedent paper, [5], we stick to this setting.

A sequence of edges that joins a sequence of vertices is called a *path*. Let $P(v_i, v_j)$ ($\subseteq 2^E$) be the set of all paths from the point v_i to v_j without cycles. I assume at least one path exists between any pair of origin and destination, $P(v_i, v_j) \neq \emptyset$ for all $v_i, v_j \in V$ such that $v_i \neq v_j$. Then, $P = \cup_{v_i, v_j \in V^2} P(v_i, v_j)$ denotes the set of all acyclic paths.

Each edge $e \in E$ has an ex-post cost function $c_e \colon [0,1] \times \Omega \to \mathbb{R}_+$ that maps from (i) a fraction of agents who use this edge s_e and (ii) the state of world ω to the travel time. We assume that c_e is independent of the shares of other edges, $s_{e'}$. A cost function represents time required to travel through edge e. We assume that $c_e(s_e, \omega)$ is non-negative, continuously differentiable, and strictly increasing in s_e.

A state of the world ω is drawn from a finite set Ω according to a full-support prior $\bar{\mu} \in int(\Delta\Omega)$. The agents cannot directly observe the realized state ω, but they know each other that it is drawn from the prior distribution $\bar{\mu}$.

A Bayesian congestion game is described as $BG = (f, P, (c_p)_{p \in P}, \Omega, \bar{\mu})$, in which agents choose one of the acyclic[2] paths $p \in P$ so that they minimize their own expected travel cost

$$E_{\bar{\mu}}[c_p(\mathbf{s}, \omega)] = \sum_{\omega \in \Omega} c_p(\mathbf{s}, \omega) \bar{\mu}(\omega),$$

where $\mathbf{s} \equiv (s_p)_{p \in P}$ denotes a vector of path shares and c_p is the travel time needed to traverse path p:

$$c_p(\mathbf{s}, \omega) \equiv \sum_{e \in P} c_e \left(\sum_{\substack{p \in P \\ \text{s.t. } e \in p}} s_p, \omega \right).$$

Here, we define an equilibrium concept of Bayesian congestion games without signals. Since all agents have the same cost (utility) functions, we focus only on the share of paths rather than agents' actions themselves.

Definition 1 (Bayes Wardrop Equilibrium). *A share vector of paths* $\mathbf{s} \equiv (s_p)_{p \in P}$ *is a Bayes Wardrop equilibrium under a common belief* $\mu \in \Delta\Omega$ *if there exists a constant* $\lambda > 0$ *such that*

- *For* $p \in P$ *with* $s_p > 0$, $E_\mu[c_p(\mathbf{s}, \omega)] = \sum_{\omega \in \Omega} c_p(\mathbf{s}, \omega) \mu(\omega) = \lambda$, *and*
- *For* $p \in P$ *with* $s_p = 0$, $E_\mu[c_p(\mathbf{s}, \omega)] \geq \lambda$.

2.2 Information Design

Given a base Bayesian congestion game BG, we introduce an information designer who can observe the realized state $\omega \in \Omega$ and send a signal $t_i \in T$ to each agent $i \in I$. We assume the signal set T is finite and nonempty.

---

[2] Since all cost functions are non-negative and strictly increasing with respect to their shares, we can restrict agents' action set to the acyclic paths without loss of generality.

Specifically, we focus on the form of policies $\pi\colon \Omega \to \Delta(\Delta T)$, which means the policy determines *a distribution of signal realization*, $\pi(\mathbf{s}^T \mid \omega)$, and then each agent receives an i.i.d. draw from $\mathbf{s}^T \in \Delta T$. Note that this definition contains both public policies and private i.i.d. policies: if π is a public policy, then $\mathbf{s}^T$ is an indicator vector

$$\mathbf{s}^T = (0, \ldots, 0, 1, 0, \ldots, 0)$$

which means all agents receive the same signal. If π is a private i.i.d. policy, then $\pi(\mathbf{s}^T \mid \omega) = 1$ for some $\mathbf{s}^T \in \Delta T$ and 0 otherwise.

After observing a signal $t \in T$, each agent Bayesian updates their prior distribution $\bar{\mu}$ and constructs a posterior over states and shares of signals, $\mu_t \in \Delta(\Omega \times \Delta T)$ as

$$\mu_t(\omega, \mathbf{s}^T) = \frac{\bar{\mu}(\omega)\pi(\mathbf{s}^T \mid \omega)s_t^T}{\sum_{\omega' \in \Omega}\sum_{\mathbf{s}^{T'} \in \mathrm{supp}\,\pi} \bar{\mu}(\omega')\pi(\mathbf{s}^{T'} \mid \omega')s_t^{T'}}.$$

After receiving signals, the agents face the induced Bayesian game $G = (f, P, (c_p)_{p \in P}, \Omega, (\mu_t)_{t \in T})$, in which a strategy of each agent is denoted by $\sigma_i\colon T \to \Delta P$. In the induced Bayesian game G, we assume that the agents play one of the Bayes correlated equilibria defined as follows.

Definition 2 (Bayes Correlated Equilibrium). *A decision rule of shares, $\sigma\colon \Omega \times \Delta T \to \Delta P$, constitutes a Bayes correlated equilibrium if for any origin-destination pair (v_i, v_j), for any two paths between them $p, p' \in P(v_i, v_j)$, and for any signal share vector $t \in T$, the following holds:*

$$\sum_{\omega \in \Omega}\sum_{\mathbf{s}^T} \mu_t(\omega, \mathbf{s}^T)\sigma(p \mid \omega, \mathbf{s}^T)c_p(\mathbf{s}(\omega, \mathbf{s}^T), \omega)$$
$$\leq \sum_{\omega \in \Omega}\sum_{\mathbf{s}^T} \mu_t(\omega, \mathbf{s}^T)\sigma(p \mid \omega, \mathbf{s}^T)c_{p'}(\mathbf{s}(\omega, \mathbf{s}^T), \omega),$$

where $\mathbf{s}(\omega, \mathbf{s}^T) = (s_p(\omega, \mathbf{s}^T))_{p \in P}$ and $s_p(\omega, \mathbf{s}^T) = \sigma(p \mid \omega, \mathbf{s}^T)$. In words, every agent has no incentive to deviate from the decision rule σ and choose another path p'.

Following the common information design framework, we assume the designer can commit to a signal structure (T, π) before observing the true state ω. The designer tries to minimize the expected total travel time of the agents

$$C(\pi) = \mathrm{E}_{\bar{\mu}}\left[\sum_{\mathbf{s}^T \in \mathrm{supp}\,\pi} \pi\left(\mathbf{s}^T \mid \omega\right) \sum_{p \in P} s_p^*\left(\omega, \mathbf{s}^T\right) c_p\left(\mathbf{s}^*(\omega, \mathbf{s}^T), \omega\right)\right]$$

where $\mathbf{s}^*(\omega, \mathbf{s}^T)$ is an equilibrium share vector. We also assume that the agents always play the equilibrium that minimizes the designer's objective function (ETTT) when multiple equilibria exist.

3 Information Design with Public Signals

This section focuses on the public signaling policy, which only sends common signals among the agents. Therefore, we can write the designer's policy function as $\pi : \Omega \to \Delta T$. In this setting, the agents have a common posterior about states $\mu_t \in \Delta \Omega$ after observing a public signal $t \in T$ as

$$\mu_t(\omega) = \frac{\pi(t \mid \omega)\bar{\mu}(\omega)}{\sum_{\omega' \in \Omega} \pi(t \mid \omega')\bar{\mu}(\omega')}.$$

Then, the agents play a Bayes Wardrop equilibrium of the game $(f, P, (c_p)_{p \in P}, \Omega, \mu_t)$, given a public signal $t \in T$.

Let **s** be a share of the paths. In fact, this Bayesian game has a potential function that characterizes its equilibrium:

$$\Phi_{\mu_t}(\mathbf{s}) = \mathrm{E}_{\mu_t}\left[\sum_{e \in E} \int_0^{s_e} c_e(x, \omega)\, dx\right]$$

$$= \sum_{\omega \in \Omega} \mu_t(\omega) \sum_{e \in E} \int_0^{s_e} c_e(x, \omega)\, dx,$$

where $s_e = \sum_{\substack{p \in P \\ \text{s.t. } e \in p}} s_p$.

Proposition 1. *Given a posterior belief μ_t, $\mathbf{s} = (s_p)_{p \in P}$ is a Bayes Wardrop equilibrium of the induced game $(f, P, (c_p)_{p \in P}, \Omega, \mu_t)$ if and only if it is a solution to the following minimization problem.*

$$\min \Phi_{\mu_t}(\mathbf{s})$$

$$\text{s.t.} \begin{cases} \sum_{p \in P(v_i, v_j)} s_p = f(v_i, v_j), \ \forall v_i, v_j \in V^2 \\ s_p \geq 0, \ \forall p \in P. \end{cases} \quad (1)$$

Proof. If part. Since Φ_{μ_t} is continuous in **s** and the feasible set is compact, this constrained minimization problem has a solution. Define the Lagrangian

$$\mathcal{L}(\mathbf{s}, \lambda) \equiv \Phi_{\mu_t}(\mathbf{s}) - \sum_{v_i, v_j} \lambda_{i,j} \left(\sum_{p \in P(v_i, v_j)} s_p - f(v_i, v_j)\right)$$
$$- \sum_{p \in P} \lambda_p s_p.$$

Here, note that

$$\frac{\partial \Phi_{\mu_t}}{\partial s_p} = \frac{\partial}{\partial s_p} \mathrm{E}_{\mu_t}\left[\sum_{e \in E} \int_0^{\sum_{p \in P \text{ s.t. } e \in p} s_p} c_e(x, \omega)\, dx\right]$$

$$= \mathrm{E}_{\mu_t}\left[\sum_{e \in p} c_e(s_e, \omega)\right]$$

$$= \mathrm{E}_{\mu_t}[c_p(\mathbf{s}, \omega)].$$

Hence, the KKT conditions for this problem are as follows:

$$\frac{\partial \mathcal{L}}{\partial s_p} = \mathrm{E}_{\mu_t}[c_p(\mathbf{s},\omega)] - \bar{\lambda}_p - \lambda_p = 0 \tag{2}$$

$$\forall (v_i, v_j) \in V^2, \sum_{p \in P(v_i, v_j)} s_p - f(v_i, v_j) = 0 \tag{3}$$

$$\forall p \in P, \; s_p \geq 0, \; \lambda_p \geq 0, \; \lambda_p s_p = 0 \tag{4}$$

where $\bar{\lambda}_p \equiv \lambda_{i,j}$ s.t. $p \in P(v_i, v_j)$.

Let $p \in P(v_i, v_j)$. If $s_p > 0$, then $\lambda_p = 0$, which implies $\mathrm{E}_{\mu_t}[c_p(s_p,\omega)] = \lambda_{i,j}$. On the other hand, if $s_p = 0$, then $\mathrm{E}_{\mu_t}[c_p(s_p,\omega)] \geq \lambda_{i,j}$. Hence the solution to this minimization problem is a Wardrop equilibrium.

Only if part. If $\mathbf{s}$ is a Wardrop equilibrium, there exist $\lambda_{i,j}$ (the common travel time from v_i to v_j) and λ_p (the share of path p) that satisfy the KKT conditions. Since Φ is a convex function ($\because c_e$'s are increasing) and the feasible area is convex, the minimization problem (1) has a unique solution. Therefore the Wardrop equilibrium is the solution to the minimization problem.

Corollary 1. *The set of Bayes Wardrop equilibria of the induced game $G = (f, P, (c_p)_{p \in P}, \Omega, \mu_t)$ can be computed by the KKT conditions. It is non-empty and singleton.*

Since the Bayes Wardrop equilibrium is unique (and thus the Lagrange multiplier $\lambda_{i,j}(\mu)$ is also unique), we can derive the expected total cost given a posterior μ, $C\colon \Delta\Omega \to \mathbb{R}$, as

$$\begin{aligned} C(\mu) &= \sum_{v_i, v_j \in V^2} f(v_i, v_j) \lambda_{i,j}(\mu) \\ &= \sum_{v_i, v_j \in V^2} f(v_i, v_j) \min_{p \in P(v_i, v_j)} \mathrm{E}_\mu[c_p(\mathbf{s}^*(\mu), \omega)], \end{aligned}$$

where $\mathbf{s}^*(\mu)$ is a unique Bayes Wardrop equilibrium share of paths given a posterior μ.

Given the expected total cost function $C(\mu)$, one can derive the optimal public signaling policy by the standard convexification approach [1,7].

Proposition 2. *The expected total cost of the optimal public signaling policy is given by*

$$V(\bar{\mu}) = \min\{y \mid (\bar{\mu}, y) \in \mathrm{CH}(\mathrm{gr}\, C)\}$$

where $\mathrm{CH}(\mathrm{gr}\, C)$ denotes the convex hull of the graph of the function C. Therefore if C is concave, then the optimal public signaling policy is the perfect disclosure policy.

By Carathéodory's theorem, the optimal public policy is expressed as a convex combination of at most $|\Omega|$ points. Still, to generate the optimal public policy, we need to compute the value of $C(\mu)$ for every $\mu \in \Delta\Omega$. Even if we divide the space $\Delta\Omega$ into a grid, the computation cost exponentially increases as the dimension of Ω increases. When cost functions are of a very simple additive form, however, we know that the perfect signaling is optimal among all public signals.

Theorem 1. *If each c_e is of the form*

$$c_e(s_e, \omega) = a_e s_e + \kappa_e(\omega) \tag{5}$$

for some constant $a_e \in \mathbb{R}_{++}$ and some function $\kappa_e \colon \Omega \to \mathbb{R}$, then $C(\mu)$ is concave in μ, which implies the perfect signaling policy is always optimal for the designer among all public signaling policies.

Proof. Given the cost function form, the gradients of the potential function becomes

$$\nabla_\mathbf{s} \Phi_{\mu_t}(\mathbf{s}) = \sum_{e \in E} a_e s_e + \mathrm{E}_{\mu_t}\left[\sum_{e \in E} \kappa_e(\omega)\right].$$

By the KKT conditions (2), we see that all conditions are linear except for the complementary slackness conditions. Let supp $\mathbf{s}$ be the support of $\mathbf{s}$, that is, the set of paths whose flow is positive; supp $\mathbf{s} \equiv \{p \in P \mid s_p > 0\}$. Let $U(\hat{P})$ is the region of μ where supp $\mathbf{s}(\mu) = \hat{P}$ for the equilibrium share $\mathbf{s}(\mu)$. Then $U(\hat{P})$ is a convex set. In such a region, the optimal travel time from v_i to v_j, $\lambda_{i,j}(\mu)$, is linear in μ.

Since $C(\mu) = \min_{\hat{P} \subset P} \sum_{v_i, v_j \in V^2} f(v_i, v_j) \lambda_{i,j}(\mu)$, which means $C(\mu)$ is the lower bounds of linear functions, C is globally concave in μ.

In this particular scenario, the ETTT of the best public policy is capped at no more than $4/3$ times that of the private i.i.d. policy. This limit strongly motivates a designer to opt for the straightforward disclosure of the true realized state, rather than calculating the complex private signals.

Proposition 3. *If all cost functions are of the form of Eq. 5, then the ETTT of the best public policy is at most $\frac{4}{3}$ times that of the optimal policy without incentive constraints. It means any policy, including the best private i.i.d. policy, can achieve only 75% of the ETTT of the best public policy.*

Proof. If cost functions satisfies Eq. 5, then the best public policy is the perfect disclosure of the state (Theorem 1). Since all agents play the ex-post Nash equilibrium after observing each true state ω, its total travel time is bounded above by $4/3$ times the total travel time of the optimal flow [10]. The ETTT of the optimal public policy is the weighted sum of the total travel time given each ω, so it is also bounded above by the ETTT of the optimal flows without incentive constraints.

Lemma 1. *Let $P(\mu) \subseteq P$ be the set of paths that are used in the Bayes Wardrop equilibrium given a common posterior μ. If $P(\mu)$ are same for all corner points of $\Delta\Omega$, then all public signaling policies generate the same expected total cost $\bar{V}$.*

Even if $P(\mu)$ are not same for all corner points of $\Delta\Omega$, $C(\mu)$ can be globally linear, as shown in Example 2.

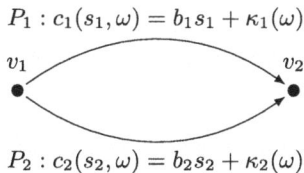

Fig. 2. A network and cost functions of Example 2. Here $b_1, b_2 > 0$ and $\kappa_1, \kappa_2 \geq 0$.

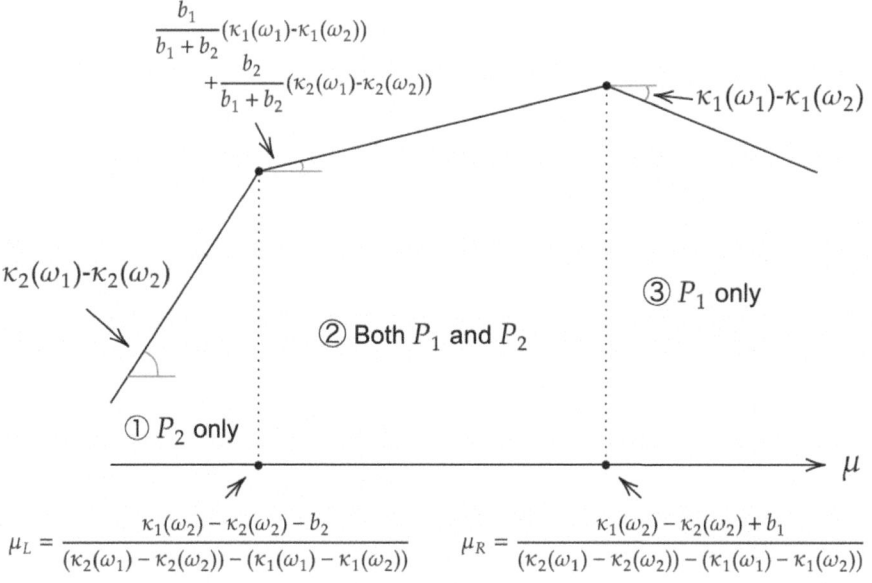

Fig. 3. Graph of expected total cost function $C(\mu)$ of Example 2.

Example 2. Consider a two edges example with affine edge cost functions described in Fig. 2. We assume that the true state $\omega \in \Omega = \{\omega_1, \omega_2\}$ is drawn from a full-support prior distribution that satisfies $Pr(\omega = \omega_1) \equiv \bar{\mu}$.

In this example, given a posterior belief μ of ω_1, the unique Bayes Wardrop equilibrium share of the induced game is

$$s_1^*(\mu) = \begin{cases} 0 & \text{if } E_\mu[\kappa_2(\omega) - \kappa_1(\omega)] \leq -b_2 \\ 1 & \text{if } E_\mu[\kappa_2(\omega) - \kappa_1(\omega)] \geq b_1 \\ \dfrac{b_2 + E_\mu[\kappa_2(\omega) - \kappa_1(\omega)]}{b_1 + b_2} & \text{otherwise} \end{cases}$$

and therefore, the expected total cost function is

$$C(\mu) = \begin{cases} b_2 + E_\mu[\kappa_2(\omega)] & \text{if } E_\mu[\kappa_2(\omega) - \kappa_1(\omega)] \leq -b_2 \\ b_1 + E_\mu[\kappa_1(\omega)] & \text{if } E_\mu[\kappa_2(\omega) - \kappa_1(\omega)] \geq b_1 \\ \dfrac{b_1 b_2 + b_1 E_\mu[\kappa_2(\omega)] + b_2 E_\mu[\kappa_1(\omega)]}{b_1 + b_2} & \text{otherwise}. \end{cases}$$

Without loss of generality, we assume $\kappa_2(\omega_1) - \kappa_2(\omega_2) \geq \kappa_1(\omega_1) - \kappa_1(\omega_2)$. Here we define two cutoffs μ_L and μ_R ($\mu_L \leq \mu_R$) by

$$\mu_L \equiv \frac{\kappa_1(\omega_2) - \kappa_2(\omega_2) - b_2}{(\kappa_2(\omega_1) - \kappa_2(\omega_2)) - (\kappa_1(\omega_1) - \kappa_1(\omega_2))}$$

$$\mu_R \equiv \frac{\kappa_1(\omega_2) - \kappa_2(\omega_2) + b_1}{(\kappa_2(\omega_1) - \kappa_2(\omega_2)) - (\kappa_1(\omega_1) - \kappa_1(\omega_2))}.$$

Then the expected total cost function $C(\mu)$ is described as Fig. 3.

Let's consider the situation in which both $\mu = 0$ and $\mu = 1$ vertical lines are contained in the region 2, $\mu_L \leq 0 \leq 1 \leq \mu_R$, as shown in the left graph of Fig. 4. In this case, for any posterior distribution $\mu \in [0, 1]$, both of two paths are used by a positive share of agents. Therefore $C(\mu)$ is globally linear in $\mu \in [0, 1]$, which implies all public policies produce the same expected total cost.

On the other hand, suppose the feasible area spans across 2 and 3 regions, $\mu_L \leq 0 \leq \mu_R \leq 1$, as shown in the right graph of Fig. 4. In this case, if $\kappa_2(\omega_1) - \kappa_2(\omega_2) > \kappa_1(\omega_1) - \kappa_1(\omega_2)$, the perfect disclosure policy achieves a strictly smaller cost than those of other public policies, irrespective of the position of $\bar{\mu} \in (0, 1)$.

In general, the perfect disclosure policy is the unique optimal public policy if and only if there exists at least one point in $[0, 1]$ where the gradient of C changes, formally,

- $\kappa_2(\omega_1) - \kappa_2(\omega_2) \neq \kappa_1(\omega_1) - \kappa_1(\omega_2)$, and
- $0 \leq \mu_L \leq 1$ or $0 \leq \mu_R \leq 1$.

Otherwise, $C(\mu)$ is globally linear in μ, so all public policies achieve the same total expected cost.

It is worth mentioning that even if cost functions are convex, the total cost function $C(\mu)$ can be concave, as illustrated in Example 3. It is sometimes optimal for the designer to send no signals (always send the same signal) to the agents.

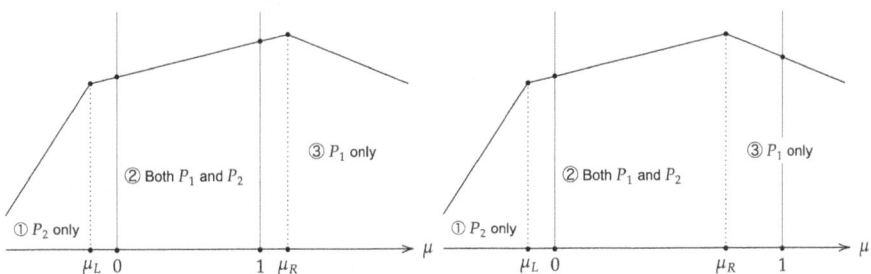

Fig. 4. Graphs of $C(\mu)$ in Example 2 when $\mu_L \leq 0 \leq 1 \leq \mu_R$ (left) and $\mu_L \leq 0 \leq \mu_R \leq 1$ (right).

Example 3. Consider a network illustrated in Fig. 5. The expected total cost function $C(\mu)$ is illustrated in Fig. 6. If an initial prior is $\bar{\mu}(\omega = 0) = \bar{\mu}(\omega = 4) = \frac{1}{2}$, then the designer will completely hide her information about states.

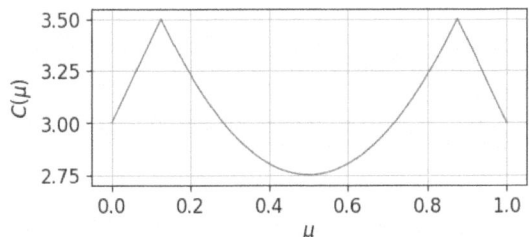

Fig. 5. A network and cost functions in Example 3. A state ω is either 0 or 4 drawn from the uniform prior.

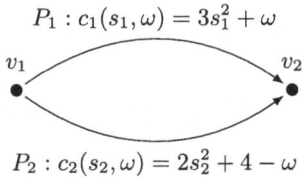

Fig. 6. The graph of total cost functions $C(\mu)$. The x-axis indicates the probability $\mu(\omega = 4)$.

4 Information Design with Private i.i.d. Signals

This section assumes that all cost functions are *convex*. we show how to derive the optimal private i.i.d. signaling policy and compare it with the optimal public signaling policy.

Table 1. The structure of general i.i.d. action recommendation policy $\pi(p \mid \omega)$ of the designer.

	p_1	p_2	$\cdots$	p_k
ω_1	$\pi_{\omega_1 p_1}$	$\pi_{\omega_1 p_2}$	$\cdots$	$\pi_{\omega_1 p_k}$
ω_2	$\pi_{\omega_2 p_1}$	$\pi_{\omega_2 p_2}$	$\cdots$	$\pi_{\omega_2 p_k}$
$\vdots$	$\vdots$	$\vdots$	$\ddots$	$\vdots$
ω_ℓ	$\pi_{\omega_\ell p_1}$	$\pi_{\omega_\ell p_2}$	$\cdots$	$\pi_{\omega_\ell p_k}$

First, we formulate the optimization problem that calculates the optimal i.i.d. policy. By the revelation principle as in [3], we can restrict the signal space to the action recommendation, $T = P$. Thus, the designer's optimal signaling policy is a solution to the following minimization problem. Here $\pi_{\omega,p} \equiv \pi(p \mid \omega)$ is the probability that the policy recommends p when the true state is ω, as shown in Table 1.

$$\min_{\pi = (\pi_{\omega p})_{p \in P}^{\omega \in \Omega}} \sum_{\omega \in \Omega} \sum_{p \in P} \bar{\mu}(\omega) \cdot \pi_{\omega p} \cdot c_p(\pi, \omega) \tag{6}$$

subject to agents' incentive constraints (ICs)

$$\forall v_i, v_j \in V^2, \forall p, p' \in P(v_i, v_j),$$
$$\sum_{\omega \in \Omega} \frac{\bar{\mu}(\omega) \pi_{\omega p}}{\sum_{\omega' \in \Omega} \bar{\mu}(\omega') \pi_{\omega' p}} \left(c_p(\pi, \omega) - c_{p'}(\pi, \omega) \right) \leq 0 \tag{7}$$

and the share constraints

$$\forall \omega \in \Omega, \forall p \in P, \ \pi_{\omega p} \geq 0 \tag{8}$$

$$\forall \omega \in \Omega, \forall (v_i, v_j) \in V^2, \sum_{p \in P(v_i, v_j)} \pi_{\omega p} = f(v_i, v_j), \tag{9}$$

where

$$c_p(\pi, \omega) = \sum_{e \in p} c_e \left(\sum_{\substack{p \in P \\ \text{s.t. } e \in p}} \pi_{\omega p}, \omega \right). \tag{10}$$

Note that (7) can be rewritten as

$$\forall p, p' \in P, \ g_{p,p'}(\pi) \equiv \sum_{\omega \in \Omega} \bar{\mu}(\omega) \pi_{\omega p} \left[c_p(\pi, \omega) - c_{p'}(\pi, \omega) \right] \leq 0. \tag{11}$$

Compared to the linear programming of the finite agents model developed by [3], neither objective function nor constraints are linear unless each cost function

$c_e(\pi_{we}, \omega)$ does not depend on its share π_{we}. This is because we consider the share of signals among agents, rather than considering the signals of each agent directly.

The KKT conditions of this constrained minimization problem are as follows.

$$\forall \omega \in \Omega, \forall v_i, v_j \in V^2, \forall p \in P(v_i, v_j),$$
$$\left[c_p(\pi, \omega) + \sum_{p' \in P} \frac{\partial c_{p'}(\pi, \omega)}{\partial \pi_{\omega, p}} \right]$$
$$+ \sum_{p' \in P(v_i, v_j) \text{ s.t. } p \neq p'} \left[\lambda_{p,p'} \frac{\partial g_{p,p'}}{\partial \pi_{\omega, p}} + \lambda_{p',p} \frac{\partial g_{p',p}}{\partial \pi_{\omega, p}} \right] \quad (12)$$
$$+ \lambda_\omega^{i,j} - \lambda_{\omega, p}^0 = 0$$

$$\forall p, p' \in P, \ g_{p,p'}(\pi) \leq 0, \ \lambda_{p,p'} \geq 0, \ \lambda_{p,p'} \cdot g_{p,p'}(\pi) = 0 \quad (13)$$

$$\forall \omega \in \Omega, \forall v_i, v_j \in V^2, \sum_{p \in P(v_i, v_j)} \pi_{\omega, p} - f(v_i, v_j) = 0 \quad (14)$$

$$\forall p \in P, \forall \omega \in \Omega, \ -\pi_{\omega, p} \leq 0, \lambda_{\omega, p}^0 \geq 0, \lambda_{\omega, p}^0 \cdot \pi_{\omega, p} = 0. \quad (15)$$

We cannot say that the feasible area is a convex set in general, so the KKT conditions might not provide a unique solution. Section 4.1 derives a sufficient condition that the objective function is a convex function and the feasible area is a convex set in the simple two-path networks.

It is important to note that the ETTT of the optimal private i.i.d. policy is always smaller than that of the optimal public policy. This is because the equilibrium shares resulting from any public policy, after sending the public signal $t \in T$, can be replicated by a direct action recommendation. Although such a private i.i.d. policy π requires $T \times P$ signal space, the revelation principle affirms that there exists a direct recommendation policy π' that achieves the same ETTT.

Proposition 4. *The ETTT of the optimal private i.i.d. policy is always smaller than that of the optimal public policy.*

4.1 Uniqueness of the KKT Conditions in Simple Networks

In this subsection, we focus on a two-edge network as in Fig. 7 and provide a sufficient condition for the uniqueness of the KKT conditions for the optimal i.i.d. policy calculation. This analysis extends the two examples in [5].

Formally let a network be $N = (V, E)$ with $V = \{v_1, v_2\}$ and $E = \{e_1, e_2\}$. We assume both edges go from v_1 to v_2, and thus $P = E$. The set of states Ω is an arbitrary finite set and the common prior distribution is denoted by

$\bar{\mu} \in int(\Delta\Omega)$. The edge cost functions are $c_1(s_1, \omega)$ and $c_2(s_2, \omega)$, where both of them are strictly increasing and convex in their own shares s_1, s_2 respectively. Additionally we assume that the difference of the second derivatives of c_1, c_2 are small compared to the sum of first derivatives, given each state $\omega \in \Omega$:

$$2\left(\frac{\partial c_1(s_1,\omega)}{\partial s_1} + \frac{\partial c_2(s_2,\omega)}{\partial s_2}\right) - \left|\frac{\partial^2 c_1(s_1,\omega)}{\partial s_1^2} - \frac{\partial^2 c_2(s_2,\omega)}{\partial s_2^2}\right| > 0 \tag{16}$$

for any $s_1, s_2 \in [0, 1]$. Note that affine cost functions as in Eq. 5 are included in this case.

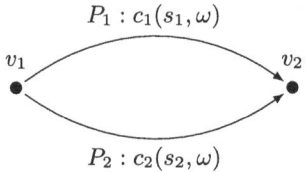

Fig. 7. A network and cost functions covered in Sect. 4.1.

The following minimization problem calculates the optimal i.i.d. policy in this environment. Here $\pi_{\omega,p} \equiv \pi(p \mid \omega)$ is the probability that the policy recommends p when the true state is ω.

$$\min_{\substack{(\pi_{\omega p}) \\ \omega \in \Omega \\ p \in \{1,2\}}} \sum_{\omega \in \Omega} \sum_{p \in \{1,2\}} \bar{\mu}(\omega) \cdot \pi_{\omega p} \cdot c_p(\pi_{\omega p}, \omega) \tag{17}$$

subject to agents' incentive constraints (ICs)

$$\forall (p, p') \in \{(1,2), (2,1)\},$$
$$\sum_{\omega \in \Omega} \bar{\mu}(\omega) \pi_{\omega p} \left[c_p(\pi_{\omega p}, \omega) - c_{p'}(\pi_{\omega p'}, \omega)\right] \leq 0. \tag{18}$$

and

$$\forall \omega \in \Omega, \forall p = 1, 2, \ \pi_{\omega p} \geq 0 \tag{19}$$

$$\forall \omega \in \Omega, \sum_{p \in \{1,2\}} \pi_{\omega p} = 1. \tag{20}$$

Fortunately, both the objective functions and the incentive constraints are convex in this setting; we can compute the optimal i.i.d. signals by the KKT conditions.

Theorem 2. *Both the objective function (17) and the incentive constraints (18) are convex. Therefore, the solution of the KKT conditions for the problem above is unique, and a unique optimal i.i.d. signal exists.*

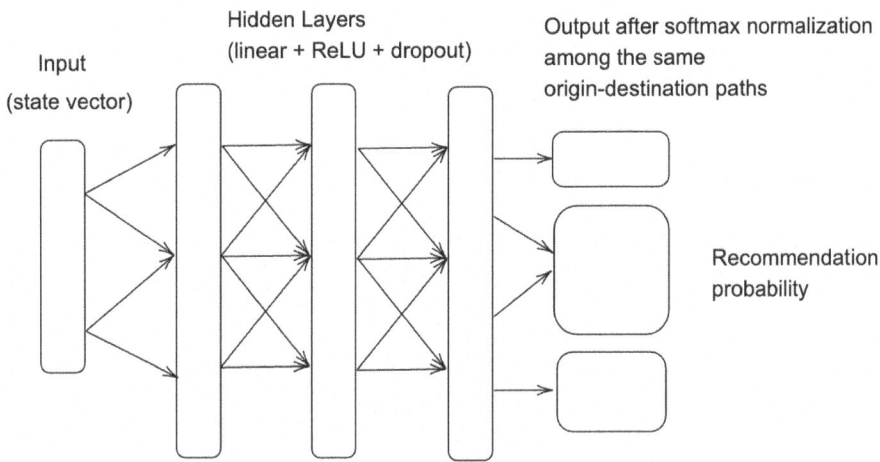

Fig. 8. A deep learning model structure.

4.2 Deep Learning Methods to Compute the Optimal Private Signal

In general, the optimization problem (6) is not linear nor convex programming, which is hard to solve. Due to this difficulty, we developed a deep learning model that approximates the optimal i.i.d. policy. It inputs a dummy of the current state ω drawn from the prior distribution and outputs a recommendation distribution after observing the state. The structure of the model is illustrated in Fig. 8. As well as RegretNet by [6] in the optimal auction literature, our model uses a loss function that is a convex combination of (i) the expected total travel time and (ii) the penalty for violating the incentive compatibility. Specifically, the model computes those terms in the following manner:

1. Randomly draw n-sample of states from the prior $\bar{\mu}$. Convert them to dummy variables (with $|\Omega|$ length)
2. Divide n-sample into batches with size k
3. For each batch,
   (a) Apply the DNN model and get the recommendation probability
   (b) Compute the ETTT by averaging k sample
   (c) Compute the IC violation $g_{p,p'}(\pi)$ (the left hand side of Eq. 11) by taking the weighted average of k sample with respect to $\pi(p \mid \omega)$
   (d) Take the weighted sum of the two errors. Adjust the parameters so that it reduces the current loss
4. Repeat the step 3, t times

I applied this method to Example 1 in Introduction. We use the model of three hidden layers with 30 cells each and train it with $n = 1000$ data and $k = 30$ batch size. After $t = 100$ repeats of optimization steps by the stochastic gradient descent algorithm, we get the policy $\pi(P_1 \mid \omega = 0) = 0.8277$ and $\pi(P_1 \mid \omega = 1) = 0.3597$, which is close to the analytical solution $\pi^*(P_1 \mid \omega = 0) = \frac{2+\sqrt{2}}{4} \simeq 0.8535$ and $\pi^*(P_2 \mid \omega = 0) = \frac{\sqrt{2}}{4} \simeq 0.3535$.

5 Conclusion

In this work, we studied an information design problem in a non-atomic congestion game on general networks. Specifically, we explore two types of signaling policies: public policies and private i.i.d. policies. First, we showed how to compute the optimal public and private i.i.d. policies in this general network setting. The optimal public policy can be solved via two steps, (i) minimization of convex potential function given the posterior belief μ and (ii) convexification over the posterior belief μ. On the other hand, optimal i.i.d. policy is not easy to solve unless it is a simple network structure. Second, if the cost functions are of separable affine form as in Eq. 5, then the perfect disclosure of the true state was proved to be the best public policy. Then, the expected total travel time (ETTT) of the agents of this policy is bounded above by $4/3$ times that of any policy, including the best private i.i.d. policy. Finally, we developed a deep neural network model to approximate the optimal private i.i.d. policy.

We show three avenues for future research. First, most of our analysis depends on the assumption of affine cost functions, although the cost functions of actual streets are said to be convex in their shares. Our analysis should extend to much general cost functions. Second, we did not discuss how much the optimal public signal is useful except for the affine cost environment. One might be able to derive the value of the private signals using the following ratio:

$$\min_{\text{all problem instances}} \frac{\text{(ETTT of the optimal public policy)}}{\text{(ETTT of the optimal i.i.d. policy)}},$$

which is similar to the Price of Anarchy studied in [9]. Third, although we focused on the static information design problem, the problem should be dynamic in real car navigation environments. In order to apply the information design to actual apps, one needs to consider the information design in the game agents sequentially arrive.

Acknowledgments. I would like to thank Michihiro Kandori for his constant support and guidance. I am also grateful to Daisuke Oyama, Kyohei Okumura, Takumi Yoshikawa, and all my friends for useful discussions and comments. This study was funded by JSPS KAKENHI Grants JP21J11717.

Disclosure of Interests. The author has no competing interests to declare that are relevant to the content of this article.

References

1. Aumann, R.J.: Agreeing to disagree. Ann. Stat. 1236–1239 (1976)
2. Beckmann, M., McGuire, C.B., Winsten, C.B.: Studies in the economics of transportation. Technical report (1956)
3. Bergemann, D., Morris, S.: Bayes correlated equilibrium and the comparison of information structures in games. Theor. Econ. **11**(2), 487–522 (2016)
4. Chau, C.K., Sim, K.M.: The price of anarchy for non-atomic congestion games with symmetric cost maps and elastic demands. Oper. Res. Lett. **31**(5), 327–334 (2003)
5. Das, S., Kamenica, E., Mirka, R.: Reducing congestion through information design, pp. 1279–1284 (2017)
6. Dütting, P., Feng, Z., Narasimhan, H., Parkes, D., Ravindranath, S.S.: Optimal auctions through deep learning, pp. 1706–1715 (2019)
7. Kamenica, E., Gentzkow, M.: Bayesian persuasion. Am. Econ. Rev. **101**(6), 2590–2615 (2011)
8. Massicot, O., Langbort, C.: Public signals and persuasion for road network congestion games under vagaries. IFAC-PapersOnLine **51**(34), 124–130 (2019)
9. Roughgarden, T.: Selfish Routing and the Price of Anarchy, vol. 174. MIT Press, Cambridge (2005)
10. Roughgarden, T., Tardos, É.: Bounding the inefficiency of equilibria in nonatomic congestion games. Games Econ. Behav. **47**(2), 389–403 (2004)
11. Wardrop, J.G.: Road paper. Some theoretical aspects of road traffic research. In: Proceedings of the Institution of Civil Engineers, vol. 1, no. 3, pp. 325–362 (1952)

Cascading Power

Thomas Ågotnes[1,2](✉) and Zoé Christoff[3]

[1] University of Bergen, Bergen, Norway
thomas.agotnes@uib.no
[2] Shanxi University, Taiyuan, China
[3] University of Groningen, Groningen, Netherlands
z.l.christoff@rug.nl

Abstract. Cascading phenomena in social networks happen when the adoption of some behaviour by initial adopters causes some of their immediate friends to adopt which again causes some of their friends' friends to adopt, and so on. Who the initial adopters are, or rather how they are positioned in the network, is of crucial importance for the potential cascade. In this paper we look at the relative importance of different agents as initial adopters in a network, for a given cascading goal such as a complete cascade: which groups of agents are *sufficient*, which groups are *necessary*, and which agents are the most *important* to have as initial adopters in order for the goal to be achieved? For the latter question, we look to cooperative games and power measures to identify agents who are pivotal for a group of inital adopters with respect to the goal. We characterise the computational complexity of resulting decision and counting problems, when the goal is represented using a propositional logical formula. We also draw connections to abduction in logic programming.

Keywords: Social network analysis · Threshold models · Cascades · Power measures · Propositional logic · Logic Programming · Computational complexity

1 Introduction

Cascading phenomena in social networks happen when the adoption of some behaviour by one or several agents (initial adopters) causes some of their immediate friends to adopt the new behaviour which again causes some of their friends' friends to adopt, and so on. *Who* the initial adopters are, or rather how they are positioned in the network, is of crucial importance for the nature of the potentially resulting cascade. For one choice of initial adopters no cascade might happen, for another a complete cascade (everyone adopts) might happen, and for yet another a limited cascade might happen. It might be that some agents often are *pivotal* for the cascade to happen – it wouldn't happen without them as initial adopters – while others do not have any effect on a cascade at all. It is important to find out who the most *important* agents are, if one is interested in triggering a cascade.

A complete cascade is just one possible goal we might have. Another might be that at least a certain individual adopts, or that one group adopts and another doesn't. In this paper we use propositional logic to formalise general cascading goals. We then, first, look at identifying which agents are *sufficient* as initial adopters in order to for the goal to be reached, and which are *necessary*. Second, we use *cooperative games* and *power measures* developed in game theory and voting theory [7] to analyse the relative importance of agents in social networks as initial adopters in achieving a cascading goal. The main idea is simple and natural: an agent is *pivotal* for a group of agents, if they together as early adopters trigger a cascade satisfying the goal, while the group without that agent do not. In game theoretic terminology, the agent can *swing* the group from *losing* to *winning*. The more coalitions an agent can swing, the more likely it is that making sure that agent is an early adopter has the effect of triggering a cascade. Different *power measures* [7] capture this intuition in slightly different ways. In particular, the *Banzhav measure* is a measure of the probability that an agent swings an arbitrary coalition from losing to winning; in our context the probability of triggering a cascade satisfying the goal together with an arbitrary set of other initial adopters.

As an example, take the network T_1 in Fig. 1 (left), and assume that each agent adopts whenever their influenceability threshold, i.e., the number of friends who have adopted, is reached, and assume that our goal is that a adopts. This will happen, for example, if both b and c initially adopt. It will not happen if only b or c initially adopts. Thus, b swings $\{c\}$ from losing to winning, or b *is swing* for $\{c\}$. Similarly, b is swing for $\{e\}$: initial adoption of e is not enough for a to adopt, but if both b and e adopt then f will adopt which means that d will adopt which means that a will adopt. d is in fact swing for the empty group: if d initially adopts then f adopts; d and f triggers e; d and e trigger c; and d and c trigger a. Thus, we would expect a measure of power or importance to give a high value for d in this network with respect to the goal of getting a to adopt.

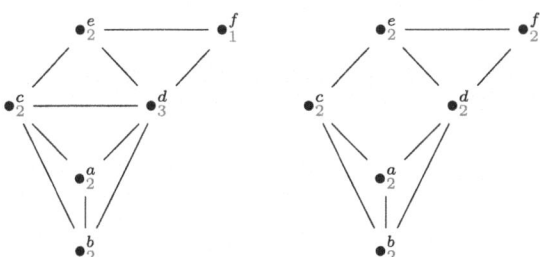

Fig. 1. Threshold model T_1 (left) and T_2 (right), with threshold values (number of friends who have adopted) corresponding to "I adopt if at least half of my friends have adopted", except for f in T_2 with a threshold of "all my friends".

In Sect. 3 we first look at the more basic notions of necessary and sufficient group of agents, and the computational complexity of deciding whether a given group, or an arbitrary group of a given size, is necessary or sufficient for a given goal. In Sect. 4 we induce cooperative games and power measures from social networks with cascading goals, and look at the computational complexity of computing the Banzhav index of an agent. These methodological approaches are inspired by work on *normative systems* (or *social laws*) [2,3]. Of course, many *centrality measures* [24, Chapter 5] of the relative importance of positions in a social network have already been proposed and studied, but most existing measures don't take the recursive effects of cascades and/or the game theoretic aspects of adopting into account – although there are exceptions [1,6,9–11,16,17,21]. See Sect. 6 for a further discussion on related work. There is also a natural relation to *abduction* in logic programming, and in particular to the *Propositional Horn Clause Abduction Problem (PHCAP)*, described as "the most elementary formalism[s] for describing systems where a propagation of values takes place and where the behavior of each single system component can be described independently of the other components" [8]. In Sect. 5 we discuss the translation of cascading problems into PHCAPs. First, in the next section, we set the stage by formally defining social networks, threshold models, goals, and cascades.

2 Models and Goals

A *threshold model* is a tuple $T = (N, E, \theta)$ where (N, E) is a social network with a finite set of agents N and symmetric social relation $E \subseteq N \times N$, and θ is a threshold function giving a threshold θ_i, a positive natural number, for each agent i. Intuitively, agent i adopts iff either (1) she is an initial adopter, or (2) at least θ_i of her friends adopt. We let $N(a)$ denote the set of neighbours (or friends) of a, i.e., $N(a) = \{b : aEb\}$. Let *cascade* be the function taking a threshold model T and a set of agents C and returning the total set $cascade(T, C)$ of agents adopting when C is the set of initial adopters[1].

Given a threshold model $T = (N, E, \theta)$ a (general) *goal* is a propositional formula over N as primitive propositions, i.e.,

$$\phi ::= p \mid \neg \phi \mid \phi \wedge \phi$$

where $p \in N$. We use the usual derived propositional connectives, such as $\phi \vee \psi$ for $\neg(\neg \phi \wedge \neg \psi)$ and $\phi \rightarrow \psi$ for $\neg \phi \vee \psi$. Intuitively a goal $p \in N$ is intended to means that p has adopted. Let $\mathcal{L}_T$ denote the set of all goals for T.

We can view a set of agents $C \subseteq N$ as a propositional valuation function $\overline{C} : N \rightarrow \{0, 1\}$: $\overline{C}(p) = 1$ iff $p \in C$. Thus, $\overline{cascade(T, C)} \models \phi$, where $\models$ denotes propositional satisfaction and where ϕ is a goal, denotes the fact that, under the assumption that agents only adopt either as initial adopters or as a result of their threshold being exceeded, ϕ will hold if the initial adopters are exactly C. We will sometimes say that in that case C is a *winning* coalition (with respect to ϕ).

A *simple goal* is a goal of the form $\phi = p_1 \wedge \cdots p_m$ where $p_i \in N$ for $1 \leq i \leq m$. We will often write, and treat, a simple goal as the set $G = \{p_1, \ldots, p_m\}$. For a simple goal, $G \subseteq cascade(T, C)$ holds iff $\overline{cascade(T, C)} \models G$.

Intuitively, a simple goal represents the agents we want to adopt. Of particular interest is $G = N$, the *complete cascade* goal, but it might be that we are only interested in

---

[1] $cascade(T, C)$ can be defined as follows. First, define $step^n(T, C)$, for any $n \in \mathbb{N}$, as follows: $step^0(T, C) = C$, and $step^{n+1}(T, C) = step^n(T, C) \cup \{i \in N : |N(i) \cap step^n(T, C)| \geq \theta(i)\}$. Finally, let $cascade(T, C) = \bigcup_{n \in \mathbb{N}} step^n(T, C)$.

influencing a certain subset of agents. Note that satisfaction of simple goals is *monotonic*: if $G \subseteq cascade(T, C)$ and $C \subseteq C'$, then $G \subseteq cascade(T, C')$. Simple goals are very natural, but also general goals are of obvious interest. For example, the goal $\phi_1 = a \wedge \neg b$ says that we want a to adopt without b adopting, and $\phi_2 = a \to b$ that we only want a to adopt if b adopts. Satisfaction of general goals is not necessarily monotonic: we can have $\overline{cascade(T, C)} \models \phi$ but $\overline{cascade(T, C')} \models \phi$ for some $C \subseteq C'$.

An example of a threshold model T_1 is shown in Fig. 1 (left). As discussed in the introduction, if $C = \{b, c\}$ are initial adopters, then a will adopt: $\{a\} \subseteq cascade(T, C)$. As an example of a more complex (general) goal, we also have $\overline{cascade(T, \{e\})} \models f \wedge \neg d$. General goals will become more interesting when we start to *quantify* over the set of initial adopters in different ways in the next section.

3 Necessity and Sufficiency

In the Introduction we observed that initial adoption by agent d in the threshold model T_1 in Fig. 1 was *sufficient* for the goal $G = \{a\}$ (and in fact also for the goal $G = N$). In general it could be that no individual agents are sufficient, but that a *group* is. In this section we look at related questions: for which groups of agents is initial adoption sufficient for our cascading goal, in the sense that the goal will be reached if we, e.g., pay them to adopt our product? For which groups are initial adoption *necessesary*, in the sense that we need them in order to achieve the cascading goal? The analysis here is inspired by the analysis of *normative systems* (or *social laws*) in [3], where similar questions are asked wrt. for which groups *compliance* is sufficient/necessary for a system to function correctly.

Given a threshold model $T = (N, E, \theta)$ and a goal $\phi \in \mathcal{L}_T$, we say that group C is *sufficient for ϕ in T* iff

$$\forall C' \subseteq N, C \subseteq C' \Rightarrow \overline{cascade(T, C')} \models \phi$$

Intuitively, this definition says that as long as C is among the initial adopters, the goal will be achieved.

For the threshold model T_1 in Fig. 1 and (simple) goal $G = \{a\}$, (minimal) sufficient groups include $\{a\}, \{d\}, \{b, c\}, \{b, e\}$ and $\{c, f\}$.

Theorem 1. *Deciding C-sufficiency is co-NP complete.*

Proof. For membership, it can be verified in polynomial time whether $\overline{cascade(T, C')} \models \phi$ for a given C' such that $C \subseteq C'$, which is enough to verify any non-instance. A naive algorithm propagates adoption until no change in at most $|N|$ steps, and in each step we check at most $|N|$ neighbours of each of the $|N|$ agents.

For hardness we show that the *complement* of the decision problem is NP-hard. The complement is the question of whether there exists a $C' \subseteq N$ such that $C \subseteq C'$ but $\overline{cascade(T, C')} \not\models \phi$.

We reduce SAT, the problem of deciding whether a propositional logic formula $\psi = (l_1^1 \vee \cdots \vee l_1^{k_1}) \wedge \cdots \wedge (l_1^1 \vee \cdots \vee l_1^{k_n})$ on conjunctive normal form (CNF) is satisfiable. Let P be the set of atomic atoms occurring in ψ. We define $T = (N, E, \theta)$, C, and ϕ as follows, and show that

$$\psi \text{ is satisfiable iff } \exists C' \subseteq N, C \subseteq C' \text{ and } \overline{cascade(T, C')} \not\models \phi \quad (1)$$

Let $N = P$, $E = \emptyset$, θ be arbitrary, $C = \emptyset$, and $\phi = \neg\psi$.

We now show that (1) holds. Note that the right hand side now is equivalent to $\exists C' \subseteq N, \overline{cascade(T, C')} \not\models \phi$. The implication towards the left is immediate: if $\overline{cascade(T, C')} \not\models \phi$ then ψ is satisfiable. For the direction to the right, assume that $v \models \psi$ for some valuation $v : P \to \{0, 1\}$. Let $C' = \{p \in P : v(p) = 1\}$. Clearly, since there are no links, $cascade(T, C') = C'$. Since $\overline{C'} = v$, $\overline{C'} \not\models \phi$.

For simple goals, however, deciding C-sufficiency is tractable, due to monotonicity.

Proposition 1. *For simple goals, C-sufficiency can be decided in PTIME.*

Proof. For simple goals G, $C \subseteq C' \Rightarrow G \subseteq cascade(T, C')$ holds for all $C' \subseteq N$ iff $G \subseteq cascade(T, C)$, by monotonicity. This can be checked in polynomial time, as noted in the proof of Theorem 1.

Correspondingly, we say that C is *necessary for ϕ in T* iff

$$\forall C' \subseteq N, \overline{cascade(T, C')} \models \phi \Rightarrow C \subseteq C'$$

As an example, consider the following model:

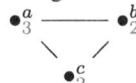

Let $G = \{a, b, c\}$. It is easy to see that the only winning coalitions are $\{a, b\}$, $\{a, c\}$ and $\{a, b, c\}$. Thus, $\{a\}$ is necessary, but not sufficient.

Theorem 2. *Deciding C-necessity is co-NP complete.*

Proof. Membership is straightforward. For hardness we again show that the complement of the decision problem is NP-hard by reducing SAT. The complement in this case is whether there exists a $C' \subseteq N$ such that $\overline{cascade(T, C')} \models \phi$ but $C \not\subseteq C'$. The proof is like the proof of Theorem 1, except that we need an extra node x: given ψ with propositional atoms P, let $N = P \cup \{x\}$, $E = \emptyset$, $C = \{x\}$ and $\phi = \psi$ (θ is arbitrary). We show that:

$$\psi \text{ is satisfiable} \quad \text{iff} \quad \exists C' \subseteq N, \overline{cascade(T, C')} \models \phi \text{ and } C \not\subseteq C' \quad (2)$$

For the implication to the right, let $v \models \psi$ and $C' = \{p : v(p) = 1\}$. $cascade(T, C') = C'$, and $\overline{C'} = v$, so $\overline{cascade(T, C')} \models \phi$. Also, $x \notin C'$. To the left: let $C' \subseteq N$ such that $x \notin C'$ and $\overline{C'} \models \phi$. Let $v = \overline{C'}$. $v \models \psi$.

For simple goals, it is less obvious than for C-sufficiency that C-necessity can be decided in PTIME. For example, there might be two winning coalitions, each containing C, where neither is a subset of the other. However, also in this case it is sufficient to check whether a single coalition is winning.

Proposition 2. *For simple goals, C-necessity can be decided in PTIME.*

Proof. C is *not* neccessary for G in T iff there is a $C' \subseteq N$ such that C' is winning and $C \not\subseteq C'$ iff, by monotonicity, $N \setminus C$ is winning. Thus, C is necessary for G in T iff $N \setminus C$ is not winning, i.e., iff $G \not\subseteq cascade(T, N \setminus C)$. As argued for sufficiency, this can be checked in polyonmial time.

So far we have looked at checking whether a given coalition C is sufficient or necessary. A more general question of obvious interest is: what is the *smallest* number of agents whose initial adoption is sufficient, no matter *which* agents we choose, for our cascading goal? How many agents are *necessary*? These questions have a direct practical relevance, in the sense that if we know that k agents are sufficient then we can just pick any set of k agents and make sure they initially adopt (e.g., by paying them); if we know that k agents are necessary then we have a lower bound on what it is going to cost us. The corresponding decision problems, given k, are k-*sufficiency* and k-*necessity*.

Given a threshold model $T = (N, E, \theta)$, a goal ϕ and a natural number k, we say that T is k-*sufficient for* ϕ iff

$$\forall C \subseteq N, |C| \geq k \Rightarrow \overline{cascade(T, C)} \models \phi$$

For example, the threshold model T_1 in Fig. 1 is 3-sufficient for the simple goal $G = \{a\}$.

Theorem 3. k-*sufficiency is co-NP complete.*

Proof. Membership is straightforward. For hardness we reduce TAUT, the problem of deciding whether a propositional logic formula is a tautology. Given such a formula, with propositional atoms P, we construct T and ϕ as in the proof of Theorem 1 and let $k = 0$. If ψ is a tautology and $C \subseteq P$, let valuation v be such that $v(p) = 1$ iff $p \in C$. $\overline{cascade(T,C)} = \overline{C} = v$, so $\overline{cascade(T,C)} \models \phi$. Conversely, if v is a valuation we let $C = \{p : v(p) = 1\}$, and $\overline{cascade(T,C)} \models \phi$ means that $v \models \psi$.

The hardness proof for k-sufficiency makes use of a general goal; we leave the simple goal case as an open problem.

We can define k-necessity in a similar way. Given a threshold model $T = (N, E, \theta)$, a goal ϕ and a natural number k, we say that T is k-*necessary for* ϕ iff

$$\forall C \subseteq N, \overline{cascade(T, C)} \models \phi \Rightarrow |C| \geq k$$

For example, the threshold model T_2 in Fig. 1 (right) is 2-necessary for the complete cascade goal.

Theorem 4. k-*necessity is co-NP complete, even for simple goals.*

Proof. Membership is straightforward. For hardness, we show that the complement is NP-hard by reducing the VERTEX-COVER decision problem: given a graph H and a positive integer k, does H have a vertex cover of size at most k? A vertex cover is a set of nodes that includes at least one endpoint of every edge in the graph. The complement, in the case of simple goals G, is that there exists a $C \subseteq N$, such that

$G \subseteq cascade(T, C)$ but $|C| \not\geq k$. Due to monotonicity the latter condition is equivalent to $|C| = k - 1$.

Given a graph $H = (V, E)$ and $k > 0$, let $T = (V, E, \theta)$ where $\theta(v) = |\{w : vEw\}|$ for all $v \in V$, $k' = k + 1$, and (simple) goal $G = V$ (full cascade). We show that:

H has a vertex cover of size k iff
$$\exists C \subseteq V \text{ s.t. } G \subseteq cascade(T, C) \text{ and } |C| = k' - 1$$

For the implication to the right, let C be the cover of size $k = k' - 1$. If $N \not\subseteq cascade(T, C)$, there is an $i \in N$ that has not adopted after the first step of the cascade. That means that i must have a neighbour j such that $j \notin C$. But also $i \notin C$, contradicting the fact that C is a cover.

For the implication to the left, let $|C| = k' - 1 = k$. We first show that[2] $N \subseteq cascade(T, C) \Rightarrow N \subseteq step(T, C)$, i.e., that if there is a full cascade it stops after the first step. Assume, towards a contradiction, that $i \in N$ adopts in the second step (but not in the first). Then i has a neighbour j, $j \notin C$, that adopts after the first step. But that is impossible since i is j's neighbour, and $\theta(j) = |\{w : vEw\}|$.

Thus, if $G \subseteq cascade(T, C)$, we have $N \subseteq step(T, C)$. Now assume that i and j are neighbours, but $i, j \notin C$. That is impossible, because then neither i nor j would adopt in the first step. Thus C is a vertex cover, of size k.

4 Cooperative Games and Power Measures

We now move on to identifying the relative power of individual agents using *power measures*[3].

A *simple cooperative game* is a pair (N, ν), where $N = \{1, \ldots, n\}$ is a set of *players* and $\nu : 2^N \to \{0, 1\}$ is the *characteristic function* of the game, assigning to every set of agents G the value 1 (G is *winning*) or 0 (G is *losing*).

Agent i is said to be a *swing player* for G (or "i is swing for G") if G is not winning but $G \cup \{i\}$ is. Let $swing(G, i)$ be a function returning 1 if i is a swing player for G, and 0 otherwise, i.e.,

$$swing(G, i) = \begin{cases} 1 & \text{if } \nu(G) = 0 \text{ and } \nu(G \cup \{i\}) = 1 \\ 0 & \text{otherwise.} \end{cases}$$

Now, we define the *Banzhaf score* [7] for agent i, denoted σ_i, to be the number of coalitions for which i is a swing player:

$$\sigma_i = \sum_{G \subseteq N \setminus \{i\}} swing(G, i). \qquad (3)$$

The *Banzhaf measure*, denoted μ_i, is the probability that i would be a swing player for a random subset of $N \setminus \{i\}$: $\mu_i = \frac{\sigma_i}{2^{n-1}}$.

---

[2] $step(T, C)$ is defined in footnote 4.
[3] Power measures measures have been induced from from network flow games [4] or from normative systems [2] in a similar way.

Given a threshold model T and a goal ϕ, the characteristic function of the corresponding game $(N, \nu_{T,G})$ is defined as:

$$\nu_{T,G}(C) = 1 \text{ iff } \overline{cascade(T,C)} \models \phi$$

From this game we get the Banzhav scores and measures for the individual agents from the definitions above. While the latter can be seen as a normalised variant of the former and have an independent interpretation as probabilities as mentioned, we will here mainly be interested in comparing the relative importance of agents in a network and will mostly refer to Banzhav *scores* for simplicity.

Example 1. Let T_1 be as in Fig. 1, and let $G = \{a\}$. We have, e.g., as discussed in the introduction, that $\nu_{T_1,G}(\{b\}) = \nu_{T_1,G}(\{c\}) = 0$ and $\nu_{T_1,G}(\{b,c\}) = 1$, so $swing(\{c\},b) = 1$. Similarly, $swing(\emptyset, d) = 1$. In more detail:

Agent i	Swing for	σ_i
a	$\emptyset, \{b\}, \{c\}, \{e\}, \{f\}, \{b,f\}, \{e,f\}$	7
b	$\{c\}, \{e\}, \{e,f\}$	3
c	$\{b\}, \{e\}, \{f\}, \{b,f\}, \{e,f\}$	5
d	$\emptyset, \{b\}, \{c\}, \{e\}, \{f\}, \{b,f\}, \{e,f\}$	7
e	$\{b\}, \{c\}, \{b,f\}$	3
f	$\{c\}$	1

Some observations:

- Perhaps counter intuitively, we included the score for agent a, who is the (sole) goal agent, in the table, and, furthermore, the Banzhav measure $\mu_a = \frac{7}{2^5}$ is neither equal to the maximal (1) or the minimal (0) values. But this does in fact make sense: initial adoption of a is of course *sufficient* for the goal, but it is not *necessary*. In fact, if d initially adopts then it does not matter if a initially adopts as well, the goal is achieved in any case. Thus, a does not have maximal power in the sense that it is not needed. It has *some* power, more precisely the power to swing *any* losing coalition. This is exactly the same power d has. Of course, it is the relative power of the non-goal agents we are mainly interested in.
- The most powerful non-goal agent is d.
- The least powerful agent is f.

Example 2. Let T_1 be as in Example 1 but now let the goal be a complete cascade (i.e., $G = N$). We now have that:

Agent i	Swing for	σ_i
a	$\{b\}, \{c\}, \{e\}, \{b,f\}, \{e,f\}$	5
b	$\{a\}, \{c\}, \{e\}, \{a,f\}, \{e,f\}$	5
c	$\{a\}, \{b\}, \{e\}, \{f\}, \{a,f\}, \{b,f\}, \{e,f\}$	7
d	$\emptyset, \{a\}, \{b\}, \{c\}, \{e\},$ $\{f\}, \{a,f\}, \{b,f\}, \{e,f\}$	9
e	$\{a\}, \{b\}, \{c\}, \{a,f\}, \{b,f\}$	5
f	$\{c\}$	1

Example 3. Let T_2 be as in Fig. 1 (right). For $G = N$:

Agent i	Swing for	σ_i
a	$\{b\},\{c\},\{d\},\{e\},\{f\},$ $\{c,e\},\{d,e\},\{d,f\},\{e,f\},\{d,e,f\}$	10
b	$\{a\},\{c\},\{d\},\{e\},\{f\},$ $\{c,e\},\{d,e\},\{d,f\},\{e,f\},\{d,e,f\}$	10
c	$\{a\},\{b\},\{d\},\{f\},\{d,e\},\{d,f\},\{e,f\},\{d,e,f\}$	8
d	$\{a\},\{b\},\{c\}$	3
e	$\{a\},\{b\}$	2
f	$\{a\},\{b\},\{c\},\{c,e\}$	4

Recall that #P is the class of counting problems associated with decision problems in NP.

Theorem 5. *Computing the Banzhav score is #P-complete.*

Proof. For membership, recall from the proof of Theorem 1 that given T, C, ϕ, $cascade(T, C) \models \phi$ can be decided in polynomial time. In order to compute σ_i for $i \in N$, consider a non-deterministic Turing machine that guesses a set $C \subseteq N \setminus \{i\}$ and accepts iff both $\overline{cascade(T,C)} \not\models \phi$ and $\overline{cascade(T, C \cup \{i\})} \models \phi$. The number of accepting computations of this machine is equal to σ_i.

For hardness, we are going to reduce #SAT [22], the problem of counting the number of satisfying valuations of a propositional logic formula $\phi = (l_1^1 \vee \cdots \vee l_{n_1}^1) \wedge \cdots \wedge (l_1^k \vee \cdots \vee l_{n_k}^k)$ on CNF over a set $P = p_1, \ldots, p_m$ of propositional atoms. Here, each l_j^i is a literal (an atom or the negation of one) and k is the number of conjuncts.

Given ϕ, we construct a model $T = (V, E, \theta)$ and a goal formula γ as follows. Let

$$N = \{p, \tilde{p} : p \in P\} \cup \{c_1, \ldots, c_k\} \cup \{s, y\}.$$

Intuitively, there is a node for each atom and its negation as well as one for each clause. The node y will be used to connect the clauses together to say that they are all satisfied, and the final node s will be used as the node for which will compute the Banzhav score (it will be swing for all satisfying valuations). To connect the nodes together we thus let E be such that (see Fig. 2):

- for each $1 \leq i \leq k$, there is an edge between c_i and each l_j^i ($1 \leq j \leq n_j$), and between c_i and y
- there is an edge between s and y.

We define θ as follows. $\theta(p_i) = \theta(\tilde{p}_i) = |N| + 1$; $\theta(c_i) = 1$; $\theta(y) = k + 1$; and $\theta(s) = |N| + 1$. A threshold of $|N| + 1$ is unsatisfiable, ensuring that adoption only flows in one direction. Thus, a clause node adopts exactly when one of its literals does, and y adopts iff each clause does and the special agent s adopts. Finally, let the goal formula

$$\gamma = \phi \wedge y \wedge \bigwedge_{p \in P} (\neg (p \wedge \tilde{p}) \wedge (p \vee \tilde{p})).$$

We can view a subset $v \subseteq N$ such that for each p_i ($1 \leq i \leq m$) exactly one of $p \in v$ or $\tilde{p} \in v$ (but not both) as a valuation, in the obvious way (treating $\tilde{p}$ as $\neg p$), and write $v \models \phi$ whenever that valuation satisfies the propositional formula ϕ. We now show that for any $C \subseteq N$,

$$\overline{cascade(T,C)} \models \gamma \quad \text{iff } s \in C \text{ and there is a valuation } v \subseteq C \text{ s.t. } v \models \phi. \tag{4}$$

For the direction towards the left, let $v \models \phi$. Since $v \subseteq C$ and $s \in C$, by the construction of the network, each c_i will adopt (at least one of the literals is in v), and thus y will adopt.

For the direction towards the right, let $\overline{cascade(T,C)} \models \gamma$. Since γ forces either p_i or $\tilde{p}_i$ for each i, and since by construction of the network neither p_i nor $\tilde{p}_i$ can be in $cascade(T,C)$ unless they are already in C, C contains a unique valuation v. Satisfaction of ϕ by C ensures satisfaction of ϕ by v, since ϕ only contains variables from v.

Finally, let the Banzhav score for s be σ_s. We claim that the number of satisfying valuations for ϕ is $\frac{\sigma_s}{2^{k+1}}$. We know from (4) that $\overline{cascade(T,C)} \models \gamma$ iff C contains a satisfying valuation. Since N contains $k+1$ nodes in addition to $\{p, \tilde{p} : p \in P\}$, there are 2^{k+1} sets $C \subseteq N$ such that $v \subseteq C$, for each valuation v. The node s is swing for all of these: no coalition without s is winning (since y requires s to adopt).

Thus, in order to compute the number of satisfying valuations for ϕ, we compute the Banzhav score of s and divide by 2^{k+1}. This reduction takes polynomial time.

Note that the construction in the hardness proof in Theorem 5 relies on using a general goal. The case for simple goals remains an open question.

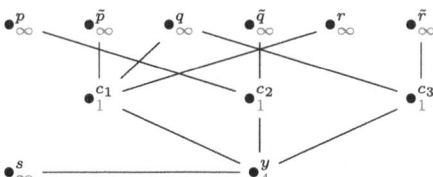

Fig. 2. Example illustrating the construction in Theorem 5 for the formula $\phi = (\neg p \vee q \vee r) \wedge (\neg q \vee p) \wedge (\neg r \vee q)$. ∞ stands for an unsatisfiable threshold (e.g., 12 in this case). Satisfying valuations: $\emptyset$, $\{p, q\}$ and $\{p, q, r\}$.

5 Logic Programming and Abduction

In this section we briefly discuss how some of the problems discussed in the previous sections can be framed as instances of well-known *abduction* problems in logic programming.

Intuitively, the threshold rule for agent a in Example 1 can be captured by the following propositional logical formula:

$$((b \wedge c) \vee (b \wedge d) \vee (c \wedge d)) \rightarrow a$$

The formula says that two of a's neighbours adopting is a sufficient condition for a to adopt, but not that it is necessary. This is what we want; a might adopt because she is an initial adopter. Observe that this formula can equivalently be written as $((b \wedge c) \rightarrow a) \wedge ((b \wedge d) \rightarrow a) \wedge ((c \wedge d) \rightarrow a)$. A formula of this form is known as a *Horn theory*, a conjunction of *Horn clauses*.

Recall that given a set of propositional atoms, a literal is either an atom (a positive literal) or the negation of one (a negative literal). A Horn clause is a disjunction of literals $l_1 \vee \cdots \vee l_n$ where at most one literal is positive. The Horn clause $\neg a_1 \vee \cdots \vee \neg a_{n-1} \vee a_n$ is written $(a_1 \wedge \cdots \wedge a_{n-1}) \rightarrow a_n$ (or $a_1 \cdots a_{n-1} \rightarrow a_n$ for brevity). A *Horn theory* is a set (or conjunction) of Horn clauses.

Given a threshold model $T = (N, E, \theta)$, we define the set of clauses $C(T)$ representing T as follows.

$$C(a) = \{\bigwedge X \rightarrow a : X \subseteq N(a), |X| = \theta(a)\} \qquad C(T) = \bigcup_{a \in N} C(a)$$

Example 4. Let T_2 be the threshold model in Fig. 1. $C(T)$ contains the following clauses:

$$\begin{array}{lllllll}
bc \rightarrow a & ac \rightarrow b & ab \rightarrow c & abc \rightarrow d & cd \rightarrow e & de \rightarrow f \\
bd \rightarrow a & ad \rightarrow b & ad \rightarrow c & abe \rightarrow d & cf \rightarrow e & \\
cd \rightarrow a & cd \rightarrow b & ae \rightarrow c & abf \rightarrow d & df \rightarrow e \\
& & bd \rightarrow c & ace \rightarrow d & & \\
& & be \rightarrow c & acf \rightarrow d & & \\
& & de \rightarrow c & aef \rightarrow d & & \\
& & & bce \rightarrow d & & \\
& & & bcf \rightarrow d & & \\
& & & bef \rightarrow d & & \\
& & & cef \rightarrow d & &
\end{array}$$

$C(T)$ explicitly tells us how adoption propagates through the network. For example, if we know that C are initial adopters, we might be interested whether that leads to a goal ϕ being satisfied. That is answered by checking whether $C \cup C(T) \models \phi$, where $\models$ denotes classical logical consequence. We might further be interested in finding the *largest* set G such that the simple goal G holds; i.e., the set $cascade(T, C)$. This corresponds to finding the (unique) *minimal model* of the Horn theory $C(T) \cup C$ [23].

If we are interested in comparing power and influence with respect to cascades, however, we want to go the other way: not from inital adopters C to final adopters G, but from a goal G in the form of a set of final adopters to possible sets C of initial adopters that will ensure that goal. This is known as *abduction* in logic and artificial intelligence.

The *Propositional Horn Clause Abduction Problem (PHCAP)* [8] is a tuple $P = (A, Hyp, Th, Obs)$ where A is a set of propositional variables, Th is a Horn theory,

$Hyp \subseteq A$ is the set of hypotheses, and $Obs \subseteq A$ is the set of observations. A *solution* to a PHCAP is a set $\Delta \subseteq Hyp$ such that $\Delta \cup Th \models Obs$.

The problem of finding out whether a given group of initial adopters is sufficient for a simple goal can be translated to a PHCAP as follows.

Lemma 1. *Given a threshold model* $T = (N, E, \theta)$ *and a simple goal* $G \subseteq N$, *let* $P = (N, N, C(T), G)$ *(the corresponding PHCAP). For any* $C \subseteq N$, $\overline{cascade(T, C)} \models G$ *iff* C *is a solution to the PHCAP* P.

For PHCAPs, *minimal solutions*, called *diagnoses*, i.e., solutions Δ such that no $\Delta' \subset \Delta$ is a solution are of particular interest (see the next section for some approaches to computing minimal solutions). That is indeed also the case for computing our power measures, for simple goals: for monotonic cooperative games the Banzhav index can be computed *solely* based on minimal winning coalitions [12].

In [8] it is shown that the problem of computing the set of *necessary hypotheses*, i.e., the set of all p such that if Δ is a diagnosis then $p \in \Delta$, can be done in polynomial time. This corresponds exactly to deciding whether $\{p\}$ is necessary according to the definition in Sect. 3. This result assumes an explicit representation of Horn clauses, while our corresponding result (Proposition 2) shows that this still holds with the more succinct representation using a graph structure. Some other results from [8] also carry over (in the case of a simple goal G): deciding whether an agent i is *possible* in the sense that it is a member of *some* coalition C such that $cascade(T, C) \models G$ is NP-complete; whether the agent is *irrelevant* in the sense that not a member of any such coalition is co-NP-complete.

6 Related Work

Conventional centrality measures from social network analysis [24] can also be seen as measuring the importance of individual agents. However, as noted in [1,11], they usually fail to take into account a node's importance in combination with other nodes. There is some existing work on measuring a node's importance when it comes to cascades. [6] describes the algorithmic problem of finding the most influential nodes when it comes to cascades, based on a Markov random field model of social networks. In [10] this problem is studied for threshold models, very similar to the models we have used in this paper (one difference is that threshold values are chosen at random). However, the exact problem that is studied is to find the most influential k-set of nodes, i.e., a set with k nodes, in the sense that when this set is the initial adopters then it maximises the number of agents adopting after the resulting cascade. This problem is studied as a discrete optimisation problem, shown to be NP-hard, and approximations are developed. With $k = 1$, this problem can be phrased as finding the most influential node. However, maximal influence in the sense of affecting the highest number of nodes when only that agent is an initial adopter is very different from being important for a cascade to succeed in general. For example, in Example 3 *all* the agents have the same influence in this sense: none of the agents can trigger a cascade *on their own*. The maximal influence approach fails to take into account the different possible combinations of other agents initially adopting when considering how important it is that an agent initially adopts.

Game theory is a natural framework for doing just that. Some game-theoretic notions of network centrality, based on cooperative games, have in fact already been proposed [1,9,16,17,21].

[1,17,21] define Shapley or Banzhav values based on cooperative games where the value of a coalition is defined by its size in addition to the "fringe" of immediately adjacent neighbours of the coalition, possibly requiring more than one neighbour in the coalition. Although this model is partly motivated by cascading phenomena [21], we argue that it does not give a good measure of cascade related power. We will use the framework in [1] to argue this point; the other mentioned approaches are similar.

The framework for defining Shapley values in [1] is parameterised by a number k, which is the number of friends an agent has to have inside a coalition to be considered to be influenced. It thus plays a similar role as θ_v in threshold models. The Shapley value for agent v_i is calculated as follows, where $deg(v)$ is the degree of node v and $N(v)$ is the set of neighbours of v, for a given value of k:

$$SV_{g2}(v_i) = \frac{k}{1+deg(v_i)} + \sum_{v_j \in N(v_i)} \frac{1+deg(v_j)-k}{deg(v_j)(1+deg(v_j))} \quad (5)$$

For comparison with our approach, since the framework in [1] is concerned with maximal influence, we set the goal to be a complete cascade. If we apply the definition above to Example 3 with $k=2$, the uniform threshold value in that setting, and $G=N$ we get the following, where the σ_i values from Example 3 are included for comparison:

Agent i	σ_i for G=N	SV(i)
a	10	0.983
b	10	0.983
c	8	1
d	3	1.07
e	2	0.983
f	4	0.983

While absolute values are not comparable, we are interested in the different rankings of importance/power. The striking observation is the strong disagreement both in the top and bottom of the ranking: a and b are ranked first (tied) in terms of importance by our Banzhav score but last (also tied) by the Shapley value; d is ranked second-to-last by Banzhav but first by Shapley. If the reader looks at T_2 in Fig. 1 (right) and is unsure what the right answer should be, consider the following: assume that all agents independently chose to be initial adopters with uniform probability. Now you can chose one additional agent to be an initial adopter. If you chose a or b, then the probability that your choice will have an impact, i.e., whether it will lead to a complete cascade that would not have happened only with the other initial adopters, is higher than if you chose any other agent. That is what our Banzhav score based ranking says. We can even quantify that probability: it is $\frac{\sigma_a}{2^{n-1}} = \frac{10}{2^5}$; around 31%. The reason the Shapley value method is not able to predict importance with respect to complete cascades better is that the "at least k neighbours" is based on only looking "one step" ahead to agents that are directly connected to the coalition in a single step. This is made explicit in Eq. (5), where we see that the value for a node is completely determined by the degrees of its neighbours – what the rest of the network looks like doesn't matter. But when it comes to cascades, it very much does.

Another idea close to ours is found in [16], which defines cooperative games where the value of a coalition is equal to the number of agents that will adopt if that coalion are the initial adopters. Shapley values are defined from these games and used to rank agents. However, this suffers from the same problem as [10] discussed above: it is not obvious that the agents with the highest marginal contributions are the most important ones for the goal of a complete cascade. In any case, they are clearly not for other goals considered in our framework, such as a cascade leading to a given agent adopting.

Our #P-completeness result for computing the Banzhav index from threshold models echoes existing #P-completeness results for counting problems related to cooperative games, including computing the Shapley-Shubik power index for weighted voting games [13], the Shapley value in weighted majority games [5], the Banzhav score for network flow games [4], and the Banzhav score for normative systems [2].

7 Discussion

Taking standard social network threshold models as a starting point, we have studied the importance of individuals – or rather their position in the network – and groups with respect to arbitrary cascading goals: whether or not an individual or group are *sufficient* for a given goal, whether they are *necessary*, and last but not least their relative importance when it comes to the probability of affecting the outcome of the cascade – by drawing on work from social network analysis, formal logic, normative systems, game theory, power measures, and logic programming. We studied the computational complexity of related problems, and pointed out the connection to abduction in logic programming. A couple of problems are left open: characterising the complexity of computing the Banzhav score, and of deciding k-sufficiency, both in the case of simple goals. Not unexpectedly, the complexity results are negative in the sense that most of the interesting problems are not computationally tractable.

An interesting direction for future work is thus to look for tractable fragments of the framework – for example restrictions on the network structure. We also leave empirical analysis and empirical comparison with, e.g., other centrality measures on network data, for future work. Here the connection to logic programming can be exploited: minimal PHCAP solutions can be computed using, for example, a linear algebra appoach [18, 20], Modelica programs [19], proof-tree completion [15] or consequence finding [14].

Disclosure of Interests. The authors have no competing interests to declare that are relevant to the content of this article.

References

1. Aadithya, K.V., Ravindran, B., Michalak, T.P., Jennings, N.R.: Efficient computation of the Shapley value for centrality in networks. In: Saberi, A. (ed.) Internet and Network Economics, pp. 1–13. Springer (2010). https://doi.org/10.1007/978-3-642-17572-5_1
2. Ågotnes, T., van der Hoek, W., Tennenholtz, M., Wooldridge, M.: Power in normative systems. In: Proceedings of The 8th International Conference on Autonomous Agents and Multiagent Systems, vol. 1, pp. 145–152 (2009)
3. Ågotnes, T., van der Hoek, W., Wooldridge, M.: Robust normative systems and a logic of norm compliance. Logic J. Interest Group Pure Appl. Log. (IGPL) **18**(1), 4–30 (2010)
4. Bachrach, Y., Rosenschein, J.S.: Computing the Banzhaf power index in network flow games. In: Proceedings of the 6th International Joint Conference on Autonomous Agents and Multiagent Systems, pp. 1–7 (2007)
5. Deng, X., Papadimitriou, C.H.: On the complexity of cooperative solution concepts. Math. Oper. Res. **19**(2), 257–266 (1994)
6. Domingos, P., Richardson, M.: Mining the network value of customers. In: Proceedings of the Seventh ACM SIGKDD International Conference on Knowledge Discovery and Data Mining, pp. 57–66. KDD '01 (2001)
7. Felsenthal, D.S., Machover, M.: The Measurement of Voting Power. Edward Elgar, Cheltenham, UK (1998)
8. Friedrich, G., Gottlob, G., Nejdl, W.: Hypothesis classification, abductive diagnosis and therapy. In: Gottlob, G., Nejdl, W. (eds) International Workshop on Expert Systems in Engineering. pp. 69–78. Springer (1990). https://doi.org/10.1007/3-540-53104-1_32
9. Gómez, D., González-Arangüena, E., Manuel, C., Owen, G., del Pozo, M., Tejada, J.: Centrality and power in social networks: a game theoretic approach. Math. Soc. Sci. **46**(1), 27–54 (2003)
10. Kempe, D., Kleinberg, J., Tardos, E.: Maximizing the spread of influence through a social network. In: Proceedings of the Ninth ACM SIGKDD International Conference on Knowledge Discovery and Data Mining, pp. 137–146. KDD '03, (2003)
11. Kempe, D., Kleinberg, J., Tardos, É.: Influential nodes in a diffusion model for social networks. In: Caires, L., Italiano, G.F., Monteiro, L., Palamidessi, C., Yung, M. (eds) Automata, Languages and Programming, pp. 1127–1138. Springer (2005). https://doi.org/10.1007/11523468_91
12. Kirsch, W., Langner, J.: Power indices and minimal winning coalitions. Soc. Choice Welfare **34**(1), 33–46 (2010)
13. Lewis, H.R., Garey, M.R., Johnson, D.S.: Computers and Intractability. A guide to the theory of NP-completeness. J. Symbolic Logic **48**(2), 498–500 (1983)
14. Marquis, P.: Consequence finding algorithms. In: Handbook of Defeasible Reasoning and Uncertainty Management Systems: Algorithms for Uncertainty and Defeasible Reasoning, pp. 41–145. Springer (2000). https://doi.org/10.1007/978-94-017-1737-3_3
15. McIlraith, S.A.: Logic-based abductive inference. Knowledge Systems Laboratory, Technical Report KSL-98-19 (1998)
16. Narayanam, R., Narahari, Y.: A Shapley value-based approach to discover influential nodes in social networks. IEEE Trans. Autom. Sci. Eng. **8**(1), 130–147 (2011)
17. Narayanam, R., Narahari, Y.: Determining the top-k nodes in social networks using the Shapley value. In: Proceedings of the 7th International Joint Conference on Autonomous Agents and Multiagent Systems, vol. 3 (2008)
18. Nguyen, T.Q., Inoue, K., Sakama, C.: Abductive logic programming and linear algebraic computation. In: Handbook of Abductive Cognition, pp. 923–943. Springer (2023). https://doi.org/10.1007/978-3-030-68436-5_62-1

19. Peischl, B., Pill, I., Wotawa, F.: Using modelica programs for deriving propositional horn clause abduction problems. In: KI 2016: Advances in Artificial Intelligence: 39th Annual German Conference on AI, 2016, Proceedings 39, pp. 185–191. Springer (2016). https://doi.org/10.1007/978-3-319-46073-4_18
20. Quoc, T.N., Inoue, K., Sakama, C.: Linear algebraic computation of propositional horn abduction. In: 2021 IEEE 33rd International Conference on Tools with Artificial Intelligence (ICTAI), pp. 240–247. IEEE (2021)
21. Srinivasan, B.V., Kumar, A.S.: Banzhaf index for influence maximization. In: Liu, T.Y., Scollon, C.N., Zhu, W. (eds.) Social Informatics, pp. 261–273. Springer (2015). https://doi.org/10.1007/978-3-319-27433-1_18
22. Valiant, L.G.: The complexity of computing the permanent. Theoret. Comput. Sci. **8**(2), 189–201 (1979)
23. Van Emden, M.H., Kowalski, R.A.: The semantics of predicate logic as a programming language. J. ACM (JACM) **23**(4), 733–742 (1976)
24. Wasserman, S., Faust, K.: Social Network Analysis: Methods and Applications. Cambridge University Press, Cambridge (1994)

Proposal of a Double Feedback Digital Product Ranking System

Yuchen Liu(✉), Rafik Hadfi, and Takayuki Ito

Department of Social Informatics, Kyoto University, Kyoto, Japan
liu.yuchen.42h@st.kyoto-u.ac.jp, {rafik.hadfi,ito}@i.kyoto-u.ac.jp

Abstract. This research proposal outlines a novel mechanisms designed to optimize the ranking order of digital products, primarily focusing on movies, TV series, and video games. The aim here is to develop a more objective quality measurement for digital products, which are typically more challenging to assess compared to physical products. The proposed mechanism, named the "Double Feedback Digital Product Ranking System", uses product's quality and customer's preferences to optimize products' listed ranking. This research relies on semantic analysis and label classification to process text reviews, and on Large Language Models (LLMs) to represent customer preferences. By refining the estimation of user preferences and product quality, online marketplaces can rank products in a more justified order for each customer, and customers will have more chances to purchase suitable products, potentially enhancing collective customer satisfaction. The main hypothesis will be tested through a multiagent system simulation that models the dynamics of the marketplace, sellers, and customers, providing a comprehensive evaluation of the system's impact on online digital product platforms.

1 Introduction

In recent years, online marketplaces such as Amazon, eBay, and Taobao have increasingly gained market shares globally. They offer a more convenient trading platform for both sellers and customers. Numerous studies and observations suggest that the current ranking of products can significantly influence a customer's final purchase decision, which, in turn, affects the profit margins of the platform and its sellers, as well as the welfare of the customers. Customers tend to view between 10 to 15 items in a lengthy list of options, as reviewing each product's detailed description on its item page requires both time and energy [1]. During this review process, customers examine various aspects of each product, including its specifications, photos, and the reviews from previous buyers. This examination helps customers form their own utility estimations, which are then weighed against the product's price to decide whether to make a purchase or not. This decision-making process underscores the critical role of product ranking in enhancing user experience and satisfaction. By understanding these dynamics, marketplaces can optimize their ranking algorithms to better cater to consumer behavior and preferences, thereby improving overall transaction efficiency and satisfaction.

For physical products, estimating utility and comparing them with other same-category products is relatively straightforward. For example, when a customer intends to buy a laptop, she can examine its specifications-such as the CPU model, memory size, and screen resolution-to estimate its utility. However, for digital products like video games, movies, and TV series, this kind of utility estimation is more challenging. The sale of digital products has increasingly shifted from physical storage media to download-based online markets [2,3]. Today, all popular game consoles offer their own online stores for game purchases and downloads, and for computer users they have options like Steam and Epic Game Store. Similarly, platforms such as YouTube and Amazon Prime Video provide services for movies and TV series. The primary distinction between digital and physical products lies in the difficulty of estimating utility before purchase or before having played or watched them. This challenge arises primarily for two reasons. First, it is difficult to create a specification for digital products similar to the laptop example. Second, much of the value of digital products is derived from the experience of playing or watching them, making it impossible for publishers to reveal all details of their products beforehand. Understanding these complexities is crucial for developing more effective marketing and ranking strategies in digital marketplaces, thereby enhancing consumer decision-making and satisfaction.

Beginning with the foundational concepts introduced in the advertisement position auction problem [4–6], where researches have primarily focused on ensuring advertisers truthfulness and maximizing platform income. Following the proliferation of online marketplaces, numerous studies have been conducted on optimal product ranking, concentrating on the utilities of the platform, sellers, and customers. A successful platform must not only secure its own profitability but also consider the welfare of sellers and customers to maintain its popularity and preserve its brand value. For instance, Chu et al. (2020) [7] developed a model to simulate an online marketplace, emphasizing the significance of providing complete product information. However, their model presupposes that each customer has a 100% chance of purchasing a product each time they make an inspection of the product list. This assumption suggests behavior more akin to planned purchases or purchases driven by specific needs [8]. In contrast, for digital products such as games, movies, and TV series, a model of impulse purchasing might be more appropriate. Iyer et al. (2020) [9] reviewed customer behavior related to impulse buying and presented a model that can somehow explain such behaviors using real market data. This indicates the need for different strategies in modeling and predicting consumer purchasing patterns in digital marketplaces, reflecting the unique nature of digital versus physical goods.

In contrast to the specifications of physical products, the quality and user preferences are more critical for digital products. Typically, the quality of a digital product is determined by factors such as its production costs, content length, storytelling, graphic effects, and soundtrack, while customer preferences focus more on the product's category, style, cultural relevance, and values (such as environmental protection, LGBT rights, etc.). Customers generally prefer to see products that align with their interests or with high quality appear at the top when they viewing product lists. If we design a customer's personal preference as a unit vector, with its direction representing his specific preferences, and a product as another vector-where the direction represents its category, style, culture, and values, and the vector length indicates its quality [10]-then the customer's net utility of purchasing a product can be modeled as the dot product of these two vectors minus the product's price. The maximum net utility is achieved when the two vectors are aligned (the angle between them is $0°$), indicating a perfect match between the customer's preferences and the product's attributes. Conversely, net utility is minimized when the vectors are diametrically opposed (the angle between them is $180°$). Also, user leave reviews based on its own net utilities, thus, with modeling of the personal user preference, we can expect a more accurate and objective quality estimation.

Currently, online digital market platforms like Amazon Prime Video and Steam employ various algorithms to rank product lists, such as clustering algorithms [11] and ranking based on release dates or product sold amount. Ranking products by release date or sales is straightforward and easy to implement. Clustering algorithms, on the other hand, analyze each customer's purchasing history to recommend products to similar customers. However, these algorithms often overlook the rich data available in customer reviews, particularly text reviews. This research aims to address this gap by harnessing the untapped potential of text reviews. By integrating customer feedback more comprehensively, this approach seeks to have a deeper understanding of user preferences and improve the overall effectiveness of product ranking systems in digital product marketplaces.

In the next section, we provide the basics of quality and preference elicitation. In Sect. 3, we illustrate the proposed marketplace simulation environment and its actors. We will cover the methodology to evaluate the marketplace environment. Finally, we discuss the expected outcomes of the research and conclude.

2 Quality and Preference Estimation Mechanism

In this section, we provide the methodology for evaluating the quality of each product and modeling the preference behavior of each customer. This includes a detailed discussion of how the entire system operates and the specific algorithms and methods that will be implemented in various parts of the system.

2.1 Overview

The primary function of the quality and preference estimation mechanism is to estimate the quality of every digital product as accurate as possible and maintain preference models for every customer who had registered on the platform. Figure 1 provides a illustration of the overall process. And each update to the system is triggered when a customer submits a new review for a product.

First, let us clarify the terminology depicted in the chart:

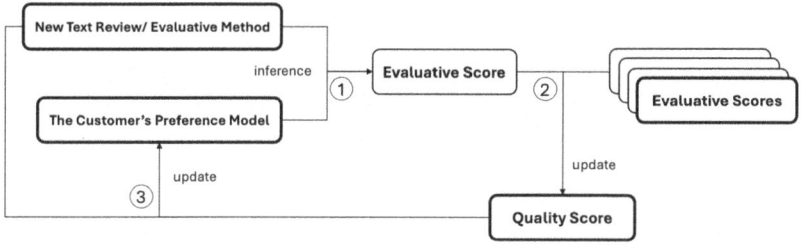

Fig. 1. Flow of the quality and preference inference in the proposed marketplace

- **Text review/evaluative method**: Text review refers to evaluations written in natural language by customers, aimed at assessing specific digital products. While evaluative method is a benchmark or rating system used by customers to measure the quality of digital products. Common examples include the 1–5 star rating system used in app stores like Apple's App Store and Google Play, as well as the like/dislike options on YouTube.
- **The customer's preference model**: A predictive model that estimates the likelihood of a customer appreciating a particular digital product.
- **Evaluative score**: A intermediate variable to store quantitative values each represents a single user's quality estimation towards a specific digital product.
- **Quality score**: This variable stores quantitative values that represent the overall estimated quality of a digital product.

As mentioned previously, each update is triggered by a new customer review, which is represented in top-left box in Fig. 1. Then in the first step, an evaluative score is derived from this new review, with utilizing the user's preference model of the individual who authored the review.

In the second step, it is assumed that the platform maintains a pool of evaluative scores collected from various users' reviews of the same product. The overall quality score of the product is then calculated based on these accumulated evaluative scores. Whenever a new evaluative score is added to the pool, the quality score is updated accordingly to reflect the change.

Finally, in the third step, the updated product's quality score and the user review are used to update customer preference model for this particular customer. This update aims to better simulate the customer's preferences for future interactions. Specifically, if a customer writes a positive review about a product that has a low quality score, it likely indicates a match between the customer's preferences and the product's category, style, etc. Conversely, if a customer writes a negative review about a high-quality product, it suggests a mismatch in preferences. This feedback loop allows for continuous refinement of the preference model, enhancing its accuracy and reliability in predicting user preferences in the future.

2.2 Text Review Processing

As discussed in Sect. 2.1, many platforms utilize various evaluative methods. However, most of these methods offer low granularity. Consider the user reviews on Google Play Store[1], Apple App Store[2], and Amazon[3]. Users can rate an app or product on a scale from 1 to 5 stars. In a scenario where we desire a higher granularity evaluative score and quality score, such as a numerical value ranging from 0 to 100, we might convert a 5-star rating to 100, a 4-star rating to 80, and so on. However, this type of metric fails to capture nuanced evaluations between scores, such as 81 to 99, which might express sentiments like "this app/product is wonderful but contains a few flaws."

To address this issue, I propose utilizing text reviews as a method for normalization and/or smoothing. This approach aims to achieve a more precise and higher granularity evaluative score for each customer review. Additionally, leveraging text reviews can mitigate the issue of users inadvertently selecting an incorrect star rating. By analyzing the detailed sentiments expressed in text reviews, we can extract subtler nuances that the star ratings alone might miss. This method not only enhances the granularity of our evaluative scores but also enriches our understanding of customer feedback, leading to more accurate and representative quality assessments for digital products.

Other platforms, such as YouTube[4] and Steam[5], offer even lower granularity in their evaluative methods, presenting a binary choice where customers can only select "like/dislike" or "recommended/not recommended" for a specific product. In such cases, processing text reviews becomes crucial to obtaining a more accurate evaluative score. The binary system significantly restricts the depth of feedback that can be conveyed through ratings alone, making it challenging to discern nuanced consumer sentiments about a product.

Moreover, there is an observable trend where product publishers and content creators prefer to shield themselves from extremely negative feedback. For example, YouTube has removed the visible count of dislikes on videos, and the App Stores do not allow users to rate an app with zero stars. These measures are likely intended to protect the reputation of products and maintain a positive user environment, but they also limit the visibility of critical consumer feedback.

As a result, the necessity for processing text reviews becomes even more pronounced. This approach is essential not only because of the low granularity of existing evaluation methods but also due to the protective policies that publishers and creators implement against extremely negative reviews. By utilizing sophisticated text analysis techniques, platforms can achieve a more detailed and nuanced understanding of user opinions, thereby enhancing the accuracy of product evaluations

---

[1] https://play.google.com/store/.
[2] https://www.apple.com/app-store/.
[3] https://www.amazon.com/.
[4] https://www.youtube.com/.
[5] https://store.steampowered.com/.

Similar to research [12]. Which did data mining to Steam player reviews to determine the "playability" of video games. In which, techniques like text semantic, and label classification are employed to determine a quantified playability value.

For the training and validation dataset, user reviews from metacritic will be employed. This platform is renowned for its extensive database of movie, TV series, and video game reviews, which includes contributions from both critic reviewers and general users. Notably, the site is particularly well-known for its comprehensive video game reviews. The dataset I collected includes all video game reviews from 2003 to 2023, with 8,372 games and over 800,000 reviews. During the model training phase, the text reviews will serve as input data, while the numerical scores provided in the reviews will act as the ground truth for regression task outputs.

One challenge in this phase is adapting the evaluative methods used in various production environments. Specifically, we must address issues such as converting different evaluation methods to a uniform numerical evaluative score and adjusting the weight of these evaluative methods alongside the outputs generated by quality regression models. This adaptation is crucial for ensuring that the models are practical and effective within real-world application scenarios, thereby enabling them to deliver nuanced and accurate assessments of digital product quality based on user-generated content.

2.3 Customer Preference Model

As briefly introduced in Sect. 1, customer preferences can be conceptually represented as vectors, and customer utility can be understood through the dot product of two vectors: one representing customer preference and the other representing digital product attributes. However, this vector model might under-fit the complexity of human preferences, considering the complexity of interests a human might have. For instance, a person might enjoy both horror movies and comedies, which could be considered as having opposite directions with vector models. This complexity indicates the challenges faced by conversational Large Language Models (LLMs), which can easily handle queries with objective answers but struggle with subjective content that varies between different user groups, such as political opinions or personal values.

To address this issue, recent research has explored aligning specific user preferences with fine-tuned language models [13,14]. Together with the publication of paper "Eliciting Human Preferences with Language Models", an API designed for human preference elicitation was published[6]. This API enables users to input descriptions and their attitudes towards content, thereafter predicting the likelihood of their interest in certain topics.

This research will employ this API or similar methods for aligning LLMs with user preferences to simulate each customer's preferences accurately. Typically, digital product publishers do not disclose complete content details, but there is

---

[6] https://github.com/alextamkin/generative-elicitation.

usually some information available about the product's themes and categories. Such details can be utilized by preference models to predict a customer's likelihood of liking a product, as illustrated in step 1 of Fig. 1. Then, in step 3, a text prompt based on the user's review and the product's quality score will be used to update the customer's preference model. As customers continue to leave more reviews, their preference models are expected to become increasingly precise, enhancing the relevance and accuracy of product recommendations and rankings. The API supports to output a probability of the customer will like a contents, which will be used in Sect. 3.

2.4 Quality Score Updating

The simplest method for calculating a quality score is to average the evaluative scores. However, this approach may not always yield the most accurate results. As demonstrated in the study "A data-driven approach for video game playability analysis based on players' reviews" [12], a running average or using weighted average of evaluative scores could be more effectively represent the "playability" of video games. In this methodology, the weight assigned to each evaluative score is influenced by several factors: the amount of time a player spends in the game, the consistency of the review (evaluated through cross-comparisons with reviews of other video games), and semantic analysis of the review text. And similar methods will be employed in step 2 of Fig. 1.

3 Marketplace Simulation

As outlined in Sect. 1, the main purpose of developing a product quality and customer preference estimation mechanism is to optimize the digital product list ranking, thereby enhancing the utility for both customers and the profitability of the platform. To test the effectiveness and value of the quality and preference estimation mechanism, I propose constructing a multiagent system to simulate the online marketplace.

We distinguish three types of agents in the multiagent system. The online marketplace/platform, the sellers, and the customers. Figure 2 illustrates how the would interact with each others by calculating their utilities and adapting their behaviors, particularly focusing on how customers decide whether to purchase a product immediately or continue browsing through the product list.

This multiagent system will allow us to observe the impacts of integrating the quality and preference estimation mechanism into the marketplace framework. By simulating agent interactions and decision-making processes, we can explore various scenarios and outcomes, thereby gaining insights into potential improvements in marketplace efficiency and customer satisfaction in the real world.

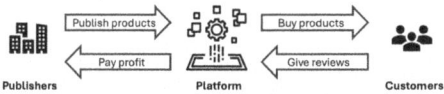

Fig. 2. Interactions between publishers, platform, and customers

3.1 Online Marketplace

The online marketplace, or platform, serves as the organizer for all digital products. Real-world examples include Steam and the Unity Game Store for video games, YouTube Primetime for movies, and Amazon Prime Video for movies and TV series. These platforms allow the publication of digital products by sellers and enable customers to browse, view, and purchase these products.

At any given time, let us assume there are n digital products defined as $P = [P_1, P_2, \ldots, P_n]$. The platform always keep a permutation function $\sigma(P_a) = b$ for each customer, where $a, b \in [1, n]$ determines the product P_a's position to slot b of the product list. For each product P_i the platform will keep a set of parameters: (p_i, c_i) where p_i is the price of the product, c_i is the commission fee to the platform of selling one of each product.

3.2 Sellers

Digital products are typically published by publishers who are responsible for various aspects of the product's life cycle, including marketing research, distribution, and customer support. However, the primary goal for these publishers is to maximize profits from their digital products. In the study by Chu et al. [7], no distinction was made between sellers and products; each publisher was assumed to publish only one product. Yet, in the real world, customers often associate brands with certain quality standards, a phenomenon known as the brand effect [15]. To more accurately reflect real-world dynamics, my simulation is going to allow each publisher to publish multiple digital products.

Let us define publishers or sellers as $S = [S_1, S_2, \ldots, S_m]$, and since publishers are able to publish one or more products, we have $m \leq n$, and $\forall P_i \in P, \exists S_j \in S$ that $seller(P_i) = S_j$, where function seller will return the publisher of a product. And publishers also have rights to set the unit price of their products. And if platform allow publishers to set the unit commission fee, the scenario would resemble an advertisement position auction [6,16]. However, consider the purpose of this research, which should focus on the effect of product quality and customer preference estimation, I propose that the product's commission fee proportional to its price, that is $\forall i \in [1, n], c_i = kp_i$ where $k \in [0, 1]$.

3.3 Customers

Modeling customers within the digital marketplace presents distinct challenges compared to modeling platforms and sellers. While the utility of publishers and platforms primarily derives from monetary profits, which are relatively straightforward to quantify, the utility for customers, especially in the context of digital products such as games, TV series, and movies, originates from the satisfaction and enjoyment derived from these products.

In several studies on advertisement positioning and product placement, customers' utility of purchasing a product is typically defined as $u_c = u - p$, where u represents the utility derived from the product, and p is the unit price. which is straightforward and easy to understand: the utility of the customer is the utility obtained from this product minus its price. To be more realistic, some models model the customer utility as $u_c = (u + \epsilon) - p$, which uses ϵ to simulate personal preference to different products, in other words, different customers may get different utilities form same product. Also, to keep ground truth utility meaningful, the ϵ usually have an average of 0.

We follow the convention with $u_c = u - p$ with u being estimated based on the evaluative score mentioned in Sect. 2.1. We define utility as $u = p_c pq$, where p_c refers to the customer preference score to the specific product, thus, $p_c \in [0, 1]$ representing the probability of the customer liking the product generated by the API mentioned in Sect. 2.3; q refers to the product's quantity, which means $q = \frac{u}{p}$ when the customer has a perfect preference match with the product. In other words, the quality of a product can be considered as cost-effectiveness of a product. And p will based on the real data set which will be introduced later. And in this research the product's utility u will depend on the product's quality and customer preference, which means different customers could get different value of u regard to the identical product.

However, the utility talked above is the exact utility a customer can get after purchasing a product. before that, we need to consider the customer's purchasing behaviour and shopping process. the basic process is simple: customer will view the list from top to bottom, and inspect each product sequentially. During this browsing process, the customer assesses each product individually. After inspecting a product-by reviewing its description, price, trailer, and other available information-the customer will attempt to predict its potential utility. This predictive utility can be expressed as in Eq. (1).

$$u'_c = u' - p \tag{1}$$

Here, u' refers to the estimation of the utility can be obtained from watch/play the digital product by the customer. Based on this, we can simulate a customer's product list viewing behaviour. Once a customer has inspected a product and estimated its utility u'_c, after that, the customer faces three potential outcomes:

1. The customer leaves the platform without buying a product.
2. The customer stops viewing and buys a previously viewed product (including the most recent one).
3. The customer continues viewing the next product.

To better simulate a human product list viewing and purchasing behaviour, the research refers to the research [7]. In the research, one important point is to prevent endless product viewing. To solve this problem, each product will be considered to have a utility cost. In this case, for outcome 1 if the customer do not want to purchase anything and leave, the net utility of this product list viewing activity is shown in Eq. (2).

$$u_{net} = -ns \qquad (2)$$

where n is the number of product the customer inspected, and s is the search cost of one product. Then, for outcome 2 the net utility is illustrated in Eq. (3).

$$u_{net} = u - p - ns \qquad (3)$$

If we consider all customers are rational agents. Then, we can consider the situation a customer just finished the inspection about product ranked at ith slot. If $\forall j \in [1, i], u'_j < 0$ and $P(u'_{(i+1)} > 0) \times E(u'_{(i+1)} | u'_{(i+1)} > 0) > s$, then the customer will choose to continue viewing the next item, otherwise, she will stop, and leave without purchasing anything. On the other hand, if $\exists j \in [1, i], u'_j > 0$ and $P(u'_{(i+1)} > max_j(u_j)) \times E(u'_{(i+1)} | u'_{(i+1)} > max_j(u_j)) > s$, the customer will also continue viewing for higher utility products. Otherwise, she will stop viewing and buy the item of index j^* with $j^* = \arg\max_j u_j$. We note that we will not consider the situation of purchasing multiple products at one time. This assumption simplifies the analysis and helps isolate the effects of product ranking and customer preference estimation on purchasing behavior.

4 Methods

4.1 Social Welfare Estimation

Once the actors of the marketplace are defined, we now look at their aggregated social welfare. Social welfare represents the combined utilities of the platform, sellers, and customers within the digital marketplace. This aggregation is quantified as a linear combination of the utilities generated by each group. For this, we define $Q = [q_1, q_2, \ldots, q_n]$ as the sold quantity of each product. We also assume that there are k product list viewing activities from all customers. The social welfare can then be defined as in Eq. (4).

$$W = \beta_p \sum_{i=1}^{n} q_i c_i + \beta_s \sum_{i=1}^{n} q_i (p_i - c_i) + \beta_c \sum_{i=1}^{k} u_{net}^i \qquad (4)$$

Here, β_p, β_s and β_c represent the weight of platform, seller/publisher and customer utilities. For the platform, the choice of β_p, β_s and β_c reflects the strategic objectives of the platform. For example, a dominant platform with a monopolistic position might prioritize its own profits, thus, make β_p higher. By contrast, a new platform seeking to attract more publishers and customers might lower β_p while increase β_s and β_c.

4.2 Simulation Dataset

To simulate the marketplace we propose to use real-world data. Although most multiagent systems do not require real data for simulation runs. the specific aim of my research necessitates the use of real data to verify the effectiveness of the product quality and user preference estimation mechanisms. Using an actual dataset of digital products and their reviews allows for the creation of more realistic publisher and customer agents within the simulation.

For this purpose, I will utilize the same data source as employed in the research "A data-driven approach for video game playability analysis based on players' reviews" [12]. Specifically, the data will be collected from Steam^{TM}, which stands as the 1st platform for PC video game retailer as of the end of 2023. Steam boasts a catalog of more than 73,000 games and has recorded over 33 million peak concurrent users[7].

Each video game on Steam is accompanied by a textual description and several tags that categorize and describe its content. Customers who purchase a game will have the right to leave a review. Each review consists of a text portion and a binary evaluative method, indicating whether the game is recommended or not recommended. Given that such binary evaluative method provide low granularity as described in Sect. 2.2, applying NLP techniques to process review texts is crucial to extracting more detailed sentiment and quality assessments. To make a more realistic simulation, the dataset will focus on video games that have garnered a sufficient number of reviews. Similarly, only customers who have left a significant number of reviews across various games will be modeled as customer agents in the multiagent system.

4.3 Expected Experimental Outcome

As mentioned above, for platforms, to gain profit, brand effect and improve their customer's satisfaction. Platforms should pay attention to the social welfare of the marketplace. Currently, for Steam platform, customers can choose to view product lists ordered by release date, number of product sold, and products based on viewer and similar customers by clustering algorithms (queue) [17,18].

The target agent platform will implement and assess these three existing ranking policies and compare them to new ranking policies based on quality and preference estimation in terms of social welfare. Additionally, we plan to explore hybrid ranking policies that combine elements of quality and preference estimation with the three traditional methods. Also the different market environments (different value of β_p, β_s and β_c mentioned in Sect. 3.4) will also be compared under different ranking policies. The expected outcome is that the platform's overall performance, in terms of both profitability and customer satisfaction, will be improved by the integration of quality and preference estimation mechanisms under different ranking scenarios and market environments.

---

[7] https://www.statista.com/topics/4282/steam/##topicOverview.

5 Conclusions

The research proposal outlines a mechanism for estimating user preferences and digital product quality, which aims to optimize product list rankings of such platforms. This method is expected to increase the likelihood of customers purchasing products that are better aligned with their preferences, thereby boosting customer satisfaction as well as the social welfare. To evaluate the effectiveness of this mechanism, a multiagent marketplace simulation system will be employed to compare various product list ranking policies.

If this mechanism proves to be successful, its application could extend beyond online digital product marketplaces. For instance, short video platforms like TikTok could integrate this system alongside AI video summarization techniques [19]. Here, AI-generated summaries could serve as input prompts to refine customer preference models, potentially enabling users to discover more engaging and relevant content more efficiently.

Currently, many recommendation algorithms fail to adequately leverage user-generated content, particularly text reviews. This research aims to tap into the untapped potential of these reviews, utilizing the rich insights they offer to enhance recommendation systems. By doing so, this approach not only improves the accuracy of product recommendations but also empowers customers by making their feedback a central element in the recommendation process.

Acknowledgement. This research was supported by JST CREST Grant Number JPMJCR20D1 and JSPS Kakenhi Grant Number 22H00533.

References

1. Kim, J.B., Albuquerque, P., Bronnenberg, B.J.: Online demand under limited consumer search. Mark. Sci. **29**(6), 1001–1023 (2010)
2. Atasoy, O., Morewedge, C.K.: Digital goods are valued less than physical goods. J. Consum. Res. **44**(6), 1343–1357 (2018)
3. Hassenzahl, M., Diefenbach, S., Göritz, A.: Needs, affect, and interactive products-facets of user experience. Interact. Comput. **22**(5), 353–362 (2010)
4. Varian, H.R., Harris, C.: The VCG auction in theory and practice. Am. Econ. Rev. **104**(5), 442–445 (2014)
5. Edelman, B., Schwarz, M.: Optimal auction design and equilibrium selection in sponsored search auctions. Am. Econ. Rev. **100**(2), 597–602 (2010)
6. Aggarwal, G., Muthukrishnan, S., Pál, D., Pál, M.: General auction mechanism for search advertising. In: Proceedings of the 18th International Conference on World Wide Web, pp. 241–250 (2009)
7. Chu, L.Y., Nazerzadeh, H., Zhang, H.: Position ranking and auctions for online marketplaces. Manag. Sci. **66**(8), 3617–3634 (2020)
8. Ahmed, N., Li, C., Khan, A., Qalati, S.A., Naz, S., Rana, F.: Purchase intention toward organic food among young consumers using theory of planned behavior: role of environmental concerns and environmental awareness. J. Environ. Plann. Manag. **64**(5), 796–822 (2021)
9. Iyer, G.R., Blut, M., Xiao, S.H., Grewal, D.: Impulse buying: a meta-analytic review. J. Acad. Mark. Sci. **48**, 384–404 (2020)

10. Petiot, J.-F., Grognet, S.: Product design: a vectors field-based approach for preference modelling. J. Eng. Des. **17**(03), 217–233 (2006)
11. Dolega, L., Reynolds, J., Singleton, A., Pavlis, M.: Beyond retail: new ways of classifying UK shopping and consumption spaces. Environ. Plann. B Urban Anal. City Sci. **48**(1), 132–150 (2021)
12. Li, X., Zhang, Z., Stefanidis, K.: A data-driven approach for video game playability analysis based on players' reviews. Information **12**(3), 129 (2021)
13. Bakker, M., et al.: Fine-tuning language models to find agreement among humans with diverse preferences. Adv. Neural. Inf. Process. Syst. **35**, 38176–38189 (2022)
14. Li, B.Z., Tamkin, A., Goodman, N., Andreas, J.: Eliciting human preferences with language models. arXiv preprint arXiv:2310.11589 (2023)
15. Faircloth, J.B., Capella, L.M., Alford, B.L.: The effect of brand attitude and brand image on brand equity. J. Mark. Theory Pract. **9**(3), 61–75 (2001)
16. Chen, Y., He, C.: Paid placement: advertising and search on the internet. Econ. J. **121**(556), F309–F328 (2011)
17. Bandyopadhyay, S., Thakur, S.S., Mandal, J.K.: Product recommendation for e-commerce business by applying principal component analysis (PCA) and k-means clustering: benefit for the society. Innov. Syst. Softw. Eng. **17**(1), 45–52 (2021)
18. Balakrishnan, J., Cheng, C.-H., Wong, K.-F., Woo, K.-H.: Product recommendation algorithms in the age of omnichannel retailing-an intuitive clustering approach. Comput. Ind. Eng. **115**, 459–470 (2018)
19. Rahman, M.R., Koka, R.S., Shah, S.K., Solorio, T., Subhlok, J.: Enhancing lecture video navigation with AI generated summaries. Educ. Inf. Technol. **29**, 1–24 (2023)

A Summary of Core-Competitiveness in Partially Observable Networked Market

Bin Li[1(✉)] and Dong Hao[2]

[1] Nanjing University of Science and Technology, Nanjing, China
cs.libin@njust.edu.cn
[2] University of Electronic Science and Technology of China, Chengdu, China
haodong@uestc.edu.cn

Abstract. We generalize the design of core-competitive auctions to encompass partially observable networked markets (PONM). Unlike traditional auctions, which often deal with scenarios of limited trading activity, our approach to core-competitive auctions for PONM captures the nature of real-world transaction markets, which is a large linking world for the economic entities and commodities circulate among the entities in the market. Our generalizing the auction market to PONM can much improve the liquidity of the auction, and is especially meaningful for the web economics. Specifically, we quantify the upper and lower bounds of the minimum core revenue in PONM, and further prove that there does not exist any truthful auction for PONM which is efficient and core-competitive. Governed by this impossible result, we identify the criteria that the allocation rule for PONM should meet. Based on these criteria, we propose a new class of auction mechanisms for PONM that is individually rational, incentive-compatible, and core-competitive.

Keywords: Core-Competitiveness · Mechanism design · Incentive compatibility

1 Introduction

In various markets, especially in larger ones, there exists an information discrepancy among economic entities. This discrepancy arises from two key factors. Firstly, economic entities often hold exclusive market-related information, such as private *valuations* of commodities or individual *connections* to others. Secondly, the vast size of the market makes it impossible for economic entities to gain comprehensive knowledge of all market participants and their connections. A typical example is online auctions, such as those on eBay, where each buyer has a private valuation for the auction item, but only a few buyers learn about/participate in the auction due to information asymmetry.

Despite having a limited view of the overall market, economic entities in these markets can still exert influence over market transactions by strategically disclosing their private information, including their values and economic connections.

For instance, visitors or bidders can use the "share" button, appearing in the upper right corner of each eBay auction page, to share the auction information with friends via Facebook, Twitter, as well as email lists. In multi-level marketing or viral marketing [8,17], each participant possesses a constrained market perception, but they hold the capability to enhance or diminish the effectiveness of marketing efforts by selectively disseminating information to others. In intermediated markets [3,5,22], intermediaries can exploit asymmetric information between buyers and sellers to facilitate trades that benefit themselves. Similar scenarios are also observed in P2P systems [10,21] and crowdsourcing markets [14,24–26], etc.

In this work, we formally define the aforementioned market as a Partially Observable Networked Market (PONM). In PONM, each economic entity "has access to" and "possesses" a segment of the market information. We study auction design for PONM, where all agents, including the seller and potential buyers, can be represented by network nodes, while their connections are edges with weights reflecting the transaction costs between agents. An allocation is represented by a simple path, with the terminal node on the path being the winning buyer and the cumulative weights of the path corresponding to transmission costs.

We design auction mechanisms for PONM which generate optimized revenue, specifically aiming for revenue that is no worse than the *core revenue*. The core revenue denotes the seller's revenue when the auction achieves its core outcome. This outcome guarantees that no subset of losing buyers can deviate to alternative outcomes that would result in higher revenue for the seller. Furthermore, in addition to optimizing the seller's revenue, core outcomes also resolve the problem of envy among bidders [11]. We extend the existing *core-competitive* revenue-optimizing auction to the intricate setting of PONM. Essentially, crafting core-competitive auctions in PONM requires striking a balance between allocation efficiency and maximizing the seller's revenue. To tackle this challenging objective, we begin by proving that there is no auction mechanism in PONM whose outcome falls within the core. Given this negative result, our focus shifts to designing truthful auctions in PONM while still preserving core-competitive properties. We affirmatively answer this question by identifying a class of truthful auction rules that exhibit core-competitiveness for PONM.

2 Related Works

2.1 Core-Based Auction Optimization

The core in the context of auctions was initially introduced in [2], where the authors proposed core-selection as a standalone auction design goal. Auctions that select core allocations generate competitive levels of sales revenues and limit buyer incentives in many aspects, which has gained popularity both in theory and in practice [1,4,6,7,12]. Within the field of auction research, studies on the core can be broadly classified into two groups. The first category investigates *core-selecting* auctions [6,7,12], which focuses on designing practical auctions that generate outcomes within the core. Goeree and Lien [12] proved that any equilibrium outcome in the core is equivalent to the Vickrey outcome. In other words, if the Vickrey outcome is not in the core, then no core-selecting auction exists. This reveals a severe incompatibility between truth-telling and core-selection. Therefore, previous research on core-selecting auctions has mainly concentrated on investigating non-truthful auctions that lead to core outcomes within the reported preferences.

In contrast, the second category of core in auctions emphasizes the importance of truthfulness and explores truthful auction mechanisms whose revenue is competitive against a core outcome [11,23]. This field of research is commonly referred to as *core-competitive* auction design, where the minimum core revenue acts as the benchmark for revenue. The notion of core-competitiveness was first introduced by Goel et al. [11], in which the authors suggested the use of the minimum core revenue as a competitive benchmark for truthful auctions. They focused on the Text-and-Image advertising setting, where there is an ad slot which can be filled with either a single image ad or k text ads, and designed truthful auctions that are core-competitive. Markakis and Tsikiridis [23] further studied mechanisms for binary single-parameter domains where each bidder's request for some type of service is either accepted or rejected, and designed the first deterministic core-competitive mechanism within the domain. Our work differs from the above work in the sense that we focus on PONM, an emerging distributed market model in which designing auction mechanisms with revenue guarantees poses new challenges, even in the scenario of a single item.

2.2 Networked Markets

Regarding the complexity of PONM, its scenarios can exhibit a wide range of diversity. In an extreme scenario, not only are buyers' valuations of the commodity and their connections kept as private information, but also the weights (costs) associated with the edges may remain unobservable. This particular setting is the most complex one, which is far beyond the existing research norms. Therefore, we explore a common setting where the edge weights are fixed and known to all participants once the edge is established. Numerous real-world scenarios align with this market model. For instance, in distribution markets like flower markets, the business relationships between suppliers and dealers often remain confidential, while transportation costs for moving commodities between locations are typically well-defined, especially when dealing with established carriers. Another example is inter-domain routing [9], where self-interested routers can strategically select paths for traffic routing and the costs of delivering the traffic along the selected path are also known. In addition, our model choice also encompasses the recently emerging diffusion auction model [13,20,29], in which the seller aims to sell items to a set of buyers who are distributed in social networks.

The closest line of research is diffusion auction design, which is initiated by Li et al. [20]. Diffusion auction is a special instance of PONM whose objective is to incentivize buyers already joining in the auction to further diffuse the auction information to other buyers via social networks, so as to improve auction outcomes. After [20], many efforts have devoted to diffusion auction design from different angles over the past few years [15,16,19,27,28,30]. For recent advances in diffusion auction design, see [13,29]. Unlike the previous work, we investigate core-competitive auction mechanisms within a more general and realistic model. In our model, the buyers' valuations are mingled with the transaction costs such that any buyer in the market could be critical, which is different from the social network settings where only cut nodes matter. Given the properties highlighted in the previous section, we believe that the core revenue can be taken as a suitable revenue benchmark for diffusion auctions and beyond.

The remainder of the paper is organized as follows. The PONM under investigation, along with the associated auction model and the notion of core-competitiveness, are formally defined in Sect. 3. Section 4 presents lower and upper bounds for the minimum core revenue. Utilizing these bounds, Sect. 5 characterizes a class of deterministic auction mechanisms, called deferred allocation auctions, that are proved truthful and core-competitive.

3 Preliminaries

3.1 Partially Observable Networked Market

Consider a seller selling a product/service in a partially observable networked market (PONM), where all agents are connected in a weighted network and can only communicate with her neighbors in the network. Besides the seller, represented by agent 0, the networked market consists of a set of potential buyers, denoted by N. Each buyer $i \in N$ has a *private type* $t_i = (v_i, r_i)$, where v_i represents her valuation on the product/service and r_i denotes the neighbors she can communicate with in the market. For each communication link (i,j) with $j \in r_i$, we use $c_{i,j}$ to denote the *transmission cost* of delivering the product/service from i to j, which is fixed and known once the communication link is established. A *transaction* in the market is defined by an agent sequence $\{a_i\}_{i=1}^{k}$ with $a_i \in r_{a_{i-1}}$, where a_0 and a_k denote the seller and the winning buyer respectively, and $\{a_i\}_{i=1}^{k-1}$ represents the selected path to transmit the commodity. For convenience's sake, we use $\mathcal{G} = (N_0, \{t_i\}, \{c_{i,j}\})$ to define a partially observable networked market, where $N_0 = N \cup \{0\}$, $\{t_i\} = \{t_i\}_{i \in N_0}$ and $\{c_{i,j}\} = \{c_{i,j}\}_{i \in N_0, j \in r_i}$. Given a PONM $\mathcal{G}$, the objective of the seller is to sell the product/service in the whole market $\mathcal{G}$, even though she can only access to a small part of entities in the networked market.

3.2 Auction Design in PONM

We model the seller's problem as an auction mechanism design. Formally, denote by t_i buyer i's true type and $\mathbf{t} = (t_i)_{i \in N}$ the type profile of all buyers. For convenience, let $\mathbf{t}_{-i} = \mathbf{t} \setminus \{t_i\}$ be the type profile of all other buyers except i. Let $T_i = \mathbb{R}_+ \times \mathbb{P}(N_0)$ be the type space of i where $\mathbb{P}(N_0)$ is the power set of

N_0, and $T = \times T_{i \in N}$ be the type profile space of all buyers. Since t_i is private information, buyer i can game the mechanism to benefit herself via strategic actions. Accordingly, let $t'_i = (v'_i, r'_i)$ be i's reported type, where v'_i represents her bid and r'_i is the reported neighbors. As buyer i can only communicate with her neighbors r_i, the misreport space of r'_i is limited to $\mathbb{P}(r_i)$. Similarly, let $\mathbf{t}'$ be the reported type profile of all buyers and $\mathbf{t}'_{-i}$ be the reported type profile of all buyers except i.

Definition 1. *Given a reported type profile $\mathbf{t}'$, we say i is a valid buyer if there exists a set of agents $\{a_j\}_{j=1}^k$ with $a_j \in r'_{a_{j-1}}$ for $1 < j \leq k$ and $i \in r'_{a_k}$.*

Given a reported type profile $\mathbf{t}'$, let $V(\mathbf{t}')$ denote all valid buyers. In addition, let Π denote the space of all possible transactions with respect to N_0 and $\Pi(\mathbf{t}')$ denote the space of transactions given by all valid buyers $V(\mathbf{t}')$. We now formally define the auction mechanisms in PONM.

Definition 2. *An auction mechanism in PONM consists of an allocation policy $\pi : T \to \mathbb{P}(\Pi)$ and a payment policy $x = \{x_i : T \to \mathbb{R}\}_{i \in N}$, and for all reported type profile $\mathbf{t}'$, π and x satisfy the following constraints:*

1) $\pi(\mathbf{t}')$ and $x(\mathbf{t}')$ are independent of $N \setminus V(\mathbf{t}')$;
2) $\pi(\mathbf{t}') \subseteq \Pi(\mathbf{t}')$ and $|\pi(\mathbf{t}')| \leq 1$;
3) $x_i(\mathbf{t}') = 0, \forall i \notin V(\mathbf{t}')$.

The *transmission costs* of $\pi(\mathbf{t}')$ is defined as $C(\pi, \mathbf{t}') = \sum_{(i,i+1) \in \pi(\mathbf{t}')} c_{i,i+1}$, where $i, i+1$ are two adjacent buyers in the $\pi(\mathbf{t}')$. The seller's revenue (or utility) can be expressed as $R(\mathcal{M}, \mathbf{t}') = \sum_{i \in N} x_i(\mathbf{t}') - C(\pi, \mathbf{t}')$. For each buyer $i \in N$, her utility function is quasi-linear and is defined as follows:

$$u_i(t_i, \mathbf{t}', \mathcal{M}) = z_i(\mathbf{t}')v_i - x_i(\mathbf{t}'). \quad (1)$$

where $z_i(\mathbf{t}')$ is 1 for the winning buyer and 0 otherwise.

Definition 3. *An auction mechanism $\mathcal{M}$ is incentive-compatible (IC) if for all $i \in N$, all t_i, and all $\mathbf{t}'$,*

$$u_i(t_i, (t_i, \mathbf{t}'_{-i}), \mathcal{M}) \geq u_i(t_i, (t'_i, \mathbf{t}'_{-i}), \mathcal{M}). \quad (2)$$

Definition 4. *An auction mechanism $\mathcal{M}$ is individually rational (IR) if for all $i \in N$, all t_i, and all $\mathbf{t}'_{-i}$,*

$$u_i(t_i, (t_i, \mathbf{t}'_{-i}), \mathcal{M}) \geq 0. \quad (3)$$

Given a reported type profile $\mathbf{t}'$, the *social welfare* is defined by the total utility of all participants (including both the seller and all buyers), which can be expressed as $SW(\pi, \mathbf{t}') = v'_w - C(\pi, \mathbf{t}')$ where w denotes the winner. Particularly, we use $\pi^*(\mathbf{t}')$ to denote the transaction with the maximum social welfare, and $\pi_i^*(\mathbf{t}')$ to denote the transaction to buyer i with the least transmission costs. Without loss of generality, we treat the seller as a dummy buyer with zero valuation so that $SW(\pi^*, \mathbf{t}') \geq 0$ for all $\mathbf{t}'$. For ease of notation, let $SW^*(\mathbf{t}') = SW(\pi^*, \mathbf{t}')$ and $SW_i^*(\mathbf{t}') = SW(\pi_i^*, \mathbf{t}')$. Accordingly, let $C^*(\mathbf{t}') = C(\pi^*, \mathbf{t}')$ and $C_i^*(\mathbf{t}') = C(\pi_i^*, \mathbf{t}')$ hereafter.

Definition 5. *An auction mechanism $\mathcal{M}$ is non-wasteful (NW) if $SW^*(\mathbf{t}') > 0$ then $|\pi(\mathbf{t}')| = 1$ for all $\mathbf{t}'$.*

Definition 6. *An auction mechanism $\mathcal{M}$ is efficient (EF) if $\pi(\mathbf{t}') = \pi^*(\mathbf{t}')$ for all $\mathbf{t}'$.*

3.3 Core and Core-Revenue Benchmark

Given a PONM $\mathcal{G} = (N_0, \{t_i\}, \{c_{i,j}\})$ and a set $S \subseteq N_0$, the coalitional value function is defined as

$$W(S) = \begin{cases} SW^*(\mathbf{t}_S) & 0 \in S, \\ 0 & 0 \notin S, \end{cases} \quad (4)$$

where $\mathbf{t}_S = \{t_i\}_{i \in S}$ denotes the types of S.

For any utility profile $\hat{u} = (\hat{u}_i)_{i \in N_0}$, we say $\hat{u}$ is *blocked by* S if there exists a set $S \subseteq N_0$ whose members can be better off by defecting the proposed outcome and redistributing the coalition value among themselves, i.e., $\sum_{i \in S} \hat{u}_i < W(S), \exists S \subseteq N_0$. The *core* is defined as the set of utility profiles that not blocked by any coalition.

Definition 7. *Given a PONM $\mathcal{G}$ and the induced coalitional game (N_0, W), the core, denoted by $Core(N_0, W)$, is defined as the following set of utility profiles:*

$$\left\{ \hat{u} \in \mathbb{R}_+^{|N_0|} : \sum_{i \in N_0} \hat{u}_i = W(N_0), \sum_{i \in S} \hat{u}_i \geq W(S), \forall S \subseteq N_0 \right\}. \quad (5)$$

By definition, any core outcome is efficient, otherwise the grand coalition N_0 blocks the outcome. If an outcome $\hat{u}$ is not in the core, then the seller can potentially raise her revenue by negotiating with the losing coalitions. This suggests that the core revenue can be taken as a suitable revenue benchmark against which to compare.

Definition 8. *An auction mechanism $\mathcal{M}$ is core-competitive (CC) if for all type profiles $\mathbf{t}$ and the induced coalitional game (N_0, W),*

$$R(\mathcal{M}, \mathbf{t}) \geq CoreRev(N_0, W), \quad (6)$$

where $CoreRev(N_0, W) = \min\{\hat{u}_0 | \hat{u} \in Core(N_0, W)\}$ denotes the minimum core revenue.

In other words, core-competitive auctions ensure that the seller obtains at least the minimum core revenue. Next, we investigate auction mechanisms with core-competitive revenues in PONM.[1]

---

[1] For any $\mathbf{t}$, the allocation that efficiently allocates the item and charges the winner the maximum social welfare is a core outcome. Thus, core-competitiveness is a well-defined concept in our setting [18].

4 Upper/Lower Bounds of $CoreRev(N_0, W)$

Before presenting our results, we first introduce a notion called critical buyer.

Definition 9. *Given a type profile* $\mathbf{t}$, *we say* i *is a critical buyer if there exists* $\tilde{r}_i \subseteq r_i$ *such that the winners in* $\pi^*((v_i, r_i), \mathbf{t}_{-i})$ *and* $\pi^*((v_i, r_i \setminus \tilde{r}_i), \mathbf{t}_{-i})$ *are different.*[2]

That is, a critical buyer is able to change the winner of the efficient allocation by cutting off some of her communication links. Let $CS_i^*(\mathbf{t})$ denote the set of such $\tilde{r}_i$ for a critical buyer i. For convenience sake we relabel all buyers such that $\pi^*(\mathbf{t}) = \{1, 2, \cdots, m-1, m\}$ where m denotes the winner of $\pi^*(\mathbf{t})$. Moreover, we use $N^*(\mathbf{t}) = \{1^*, 2^*, \cdots, (p-1)^*, p^* = m\} \subseteq \pi^*(\mathbf{t})$ to denote the ordered set of all critical buyers $\{i^*\}_{i=1}^{p-1}$ and the buyer m, where the label is given by each buyer's position in $\pi^*(\mathbf{t})$.

Theorem 1. *Given any type profile* $\mathbf{t}$ *and the induced coalitional game* (N_0, W), *we have that*

$$SW^*(\mathbf{t}_{-\pi^*}) \leq CoreRev(N_0, W) \leq SW^*(\mathbf{t}_{-1^*}). \tag{7}$$

Our next result shows that there is no IC auction mechanism in PONM whose outcome is always in the core, which motivates the exploration of core-competitiveness by giving up on exact social welfare maximization.

Theorem 2. *No auction in PONM is IC and always generates core outcomes.*

Algorithm 1: Deferred Allocation Auction (DAA)

---
1 **Input:** link function profile δ, reported type profile $\mathbf{t}'$
2 **Output:** $(\pi(\mathbf{t}'), x(\mathbf{t}'))$
3 initialize $\pi(\mathbf{t}') = \emptyset$, and $x_i(\mathbf{t}') = 0$ for all $i \in N$;
4 identify the efficient transaction $\pi^*(\mathbf{t}') = \{1, 2, \cdots, m\}$ and compute the associated social welfare $SW^*(\mathbf{t}')$;
5 **return** $(\pi(\mathbf{t}'), x(\mathbf{t}'))$ if $SW^*(\mathbf{t}') \leq 0$;
6 **for** $i \leftarrow 1$ **to** m **do**
7   compute $\delta_i(\mathbf{t}')$;
8   **if** i wins in $\pi^*(\mathbf{t}'_{-\delta_i})$ **then**
9   update $\pi(\mathbf{t}')$ by $\pi_i^*(\mathbf{t}'_{-\delta_i})$ and $x_i(\mathbf{t}')$ by $SW^*(\mathbf{t}'_{-i}) + C_i^*(\mathbf{t}'_{-\delta_i})$;
10   identify all i's critical opponents $CO_i^*(\delta, \mathbf{t}')$;
11   **for** $j \in CO_i^*(\delta, \mathbf{t}')$ **do**
12   update $x_i(\mathbf{t}')$ by $\max\{x_i(\mathbf{t}'), SW_j^*(\mathbf{t}'_{-\delta_j}) + C_i^*(\mathbf{t}'_{-\delta_j})\}$;
13   **return** $(\pi(\mathbf{t}'), x(\mathbf{t}'))$;
14   update $x_i(\mathbf{t}')$ by $SW^*(\mathbf{t}'_{-i}) - SW^*(\mathbf{t}'_{-\delta_i})$;
15 **return** $(\pi(\mathbf{t}'), x(\mathbf{t}'))$;

---

[2] In the case of multiple efficient transactions, a lexicographical rule based on the agent's unique identifier is used to break the tie.

5 Deferred Allocation Auction

We next characterize a set of novel auctions in PONM that are NW, IC, IR and CC. Before presenting our main results, we first introduce two important concepts.

Definition 10. *Given buyer $i \in N$, let $\delta_i : T \to \mathbb{P}(N)$ be a link function for i, such that given any reported type profile $\mathbf{t}'$, $\delta_i(\mathbf{t}') \subseteq r'_i$ outputs a subset of the reported communication links of buyer i.*

For convenience, let $\delta = (\delta_i)_{i \in N}$ denote the link function profile of all buyers. In addition, let $\mathbf{t}'_{-\delta_i} = ((v'_i, r'_i \setminus \delta_i(\mathbf{t}')), \mathbf{t}'_{-i})$ denote the updated type profile after removing the selected links $\{(i,j)\}_{j \in \delta_i(\mathbf{t}')}$ from $\mathbf{t}'$.

Definition 11. *Given a δ and $\mathbf{t}'$, buyer $j \in \pi_i^*(\mathbf{t}')$ is called a critical opponent of i if $\pi_i^*(\mathbf{t}'_{-\delta_j})$ is the transaction with the highest social welfare under $\mathbf{t}'_{-\delta_j}$ and is the unique transaction whose social welfare is no less than that given in $\pi_j^*(\mathbf{t}'_{-\delta_j})$.*

For convenience, let $\text{CO}_i^*(\mathbf{t}', \delta)$ denote all i's critical opponents under $\mathbf{t}'$ and δ. Based on the concepts of link function and critical opponent, we now characterize a set of auction mechanisms for PONM in Algorithm 1.

Definition 12. *For any two type profiles $\mathbf{t} = ((v_i, r_i), \mathbf{t}_{-i})$ and $\tilde{\mathbf{t}} = ((v_i, \tilde{r}_i), \mathbf{t}_{-i})$ such that $i \in \pi^*(\mathbf{t}) \cap \pi^*(\tilde{\mathbf{t}})$, δ_i is monotonic (MN) if $\tilde{r}_i \subseteq r_i$ then $V(\tilde{\mathbf{t}}_{-\delta_i}) \subseteq V(\mathbf{t}_{-\delta_i})$.*

Definition 13. *For any type profile $\mathbf{t}$, and two buyers $i \in \pi_w^*(\mathbf{t})$, $j \in \pi_m^*(\mathbf{t}) \setminus \pi_w^*(\mathbf{t})$, δ_i is strategy independent (SI) if $\delta_i(\mathbf{t}) = \delta_i(\tilde{\mathbf{t}})$ for all $\tilde{\mathbf{t}} = (t'_j, \mathbf{t}_{-j})$ where $i, j \in \pi_{\tilde{m}}^*(\tilde{\mathbf{t}})$.*

Definition 14. *For any type profile $\mathbf{t}$ and $i \in \pi^*(\mathbf{t})$, δ_i is path blocking (PB) if there is no transaction path from i to m under $\mathbf{t}_{-\delta_i}$.*

Theorem 3. *If δ is monotonic, strategy independent and path blocking, then DAA is individually rational, incentive-compatible and core-competitive.*

According to Algorithm 1, we know that the allocation policy of DAA is not efficient, that is it does not always allocate the commodity to maximize the social welfare. However, our next result shows that the auction outcome must be in the core whenever it produces an efficient allocation.

Proposition 1. *Given a type profile $\mathbf{t}$ and a δ satisfying MN, SI and PB, if $\pi(\mathbf{t}) = \pi^*(\mathbf{t})$, then $(u_i(\mathbf{t}, DAA))_{i \in N_0} \in Core(N_0, W)$.*

6 Conclusions and Future Work

This study explored the feasibility of designing auction mechanisms in PONM that generate a revenue competitive against the core revenue. We provided an affirmative answer to this question, by characterizing a class of incentive-compatible auction rules with the core-competitiveness property. This research opens up avenues for further investigation and poses several intriguing research questions. One immediate extension is core-competitive auctions in more general auction settings, such as package auctions in PONM. Exploring the challenges of designing auctions in these contexts can provide valuable insights into the feasibility and mechanisms for achieving core-competitive outcomes. Additionally, it is also interesting to explore non-truthful auctions whose outcome is always in the core with respect to the reported types. Investigating such auction mechanisms and analyzing their properties can deepen our understanding of the strategic behavior of participants and offer alternative approaches to achieving core outcomes in PONM.

Acknowledgement. This work was supported by the National Natural Science Foundation of China (No. 62202229 and No. 71601029).

References

1. Ausubel, L.M., Baranov, O.: Core-selecting auctions with incomplete information. Internat. J. Game Theory **49**(1), 251–273 (2020). https://doi.org/10.1007/s00182-019-00691-3
2. Ausubel, L.M., Milgrom, P.R.: Ascending auctions with package bidding. B.E. J. Theor. Econ. **1**(1), 20011001 (2002).https://doi.org/10.2202/1534-5963.1019
3. Blume, L.E., Easley, D., Kleinberg, J., Tardos, E.: Trading networks with price-setting agents. Games Econom. Behav. **67**(1), 36–50 (2009). https://doi.org/10.1016/j.geb.2008.12.002
4. Bünz, B., Lubin, B., Seuken, S.: Designing core-selecting payment rules: a computational search approach. Inf. Syst. Res. **33**(4), 1157–1173 (2022). https://doi.org/10.1287/isre.2022.1108
5. Condorelli, D., Galeotti, A., Skreta, V.: Selling through referrals. J. Econ. Manag. Strategy **27**(4), 669–685 (2018). https://doi.org/10.1111/jems.12251
6. Day, R., Milgrom, P.: Core-selecting package auctions. Internat. J. Game Theory **36**(3–4), 393–407 (2008). https://doi.org/10.1007/s00182-007-0100-7
7. Day, R.W., Cramton, P.: Quadratic core-selecting payment rules for combinatorial auctions. Oper. Res. **60**(3), 588–603 (2012). https://doi.org/10.1287/opre.1110.1024
8. Emek, Y., Karidi, R., Tennenholtz, M., Zohar, A.: Mechanisms for multi-level marketing. In: Proceedings of the 12th ACM Conference on Electronic Commerce, pp. 209–218. ACM (2011). https://doi.org/10.1145/1993574.1993606
9. Feigenbaum, J., Shenker, S.: Distributed algorithmic mechanism design: recent results and future directions. In: Proceedings of the 6th International Workshop on Discrete Algorithms and Methods for Mobile Computing and Communications, pp. 1–13 (2002). https://doi.org/10.1145/570810.570812
10. Feldman, M., Chuang, J., Stoica, I., Shenker, S.: Hidden-action in multi-hop routing. In: Proceedings of the 6th ACM Conference on Electronic Commerce, pp. 117–126 (2005). https://doi.org/10.1145/1064009.1064022
11. Goel, G., Khani, M.R., Leme, R.P.: Core-competitive auctions. In: Proceedings of the 16th ACM Conference on Economics and Computation, pp. 149–166 (2015). https://doi.org/10.1145/2764468.2764502

12. Goeree, J.K., Lien, Y.: On the impossibility of core-selecting auctions. Theor. Econ. **11**(1), 41–52 (2016). https://doi.org/10.3982/TE1198
13. Guo, Y., Hao, D.: Emerging methods of auction design in social networks. In: Proceedings of the 30th International Joint Conference on Artificial Intelligence, pp. 4434–4441 (2021). https://doi.org/10.24963/ijcai.2021/605
14. Hettiachchi, D., Kostakos, V., Goncalves, J.: A survey on task assignment in crowdsourcing. ACM Comput. Surv. **55**(3) (2022). https://doi.org/10.1145/3494522
15. Kawasaki, T., Barrot, N., Takanashi, S., Todo, T., Yokoo, M.: Strategy-proof and non-wasteful multi-unit auction via social network. In: Proceedings of the AAAI Conference on Artificial Intelligence, pp. 2062–2069 (2020). https://doi.org/10.1609/aaai.v34i02.5579
16. Lee, J.: Mechanisms with referrals: VCG mechanisms and multilevel mechanisms. In: Available at SSRN: https://ssrn.com/abstract=2987761 (2017). https://doi.org/10.2139/ssrn.2987761
17. Leskovec, J., Adamic, L.A., Huberman, B.A.: The dynamics of viral marketing. In: Proceedings of the 7th ACM Conference on Electronic Commerce, pp. 228–237 (2006). https://doi.org/10.1145/1134707.1134732
18. Li, B., Hao, D.: Core-competitiveness in partially observable networked market. In: Proceedings of the ACM on Web Conference 2024, pp. 156–166 (2024). https://doi.org/10.1145/3589334.3645555
19. Li, B., Hao, D., Zhao, D., Yokoo, M.: Diffusion and auction on graphs. In: Proceedings of the 28th International Joint Conference on Artificial Intelligence, pp. 435–441 (2019). https://doi.org/10.24963/IJCAI.2019/62
20. Li, B., Hao, D., Zhao, D., Zhou, T.: Mechanism design in social networks. In: Proceedings of the 31st AAAI Conference on Artificial Intelligence, pp. 586–592 (2017). https://doi.org/10.5555/3298239.3298326
21. Li, C., Yu, B., Sycara, K.: An incentive mechanism for message relaying in unstructured peer-to-peer systems. Electron. Commer. Res. Appl. **8**(6), 315–326 (2009). https://doi.org/10.1016/j.elerap.2009.04.007
22. Manea, M.: Intermediation and resale in networks. J. Polit. Econ. **126**(3), 1250–1301 (2018). https://doi.org/10.1086/697205
23. Markakis, E., Tsikiridis, A.: On core-selecting and core-competitive mechanisms for binary single-parameter auctions. In: Caragiannis, I., Mirrokni, V., Nikolova, E. (eds.) WINE 2019. LNCS, vol. 11920, pp. 271–285. Springer, Cham (2019). https://doi.org/10.1007/978-3-030-35389-6_20
24. Pickard, G., et al.: Time-critical social mobilization. Science **334**(6055), 509–512 (2011). https://doi.org/10.1126/SCIENCE.1205869
25. Shi, Q., Hao, D.: Social sourcing: incorporating social networks into crowdsourcing contest design. IEEE/ACM Trans. Networking **31**(4), 1535–1549 (2023). https://doi.org/10.1109/TNET.2022.3223367
26. Singer, Y., Mittal, M.: Pricing mechanisms for crowdsourcing markets. In: Proceedings of the 22nd International Conference on World Wide Web, pp. 1157–1166 (2013). https://doi.org/10.1145/2488388.2488489
27. Xiao, M., Song, Y., Khoussainov, B.: Multi-unit auction in social networks with budgets. In: Proceedings of the AAAI Conference on Artificial Intelligence, pp. 5228–5235 (2022). https://doi.org/10.1609/aaai.v36i5.20458
28. Zhang, W., Zhao, D., Zhang, Y.: Incentivize diffusion with fair rewards. In: Proceedings of the 24th European Conference on Artificial Intelligence, pp. 251–258 (2020). https://doi.org/10.3233/FAIA200095

29. Zhao, D.: Mechanism design powered by social interactions. In: Proceedings of the 20th International Conference on Autonomous Agents and MultiAgent Systems, pp. 63—67 (2021). https://doi.org/10.5555/3463952.3463965
30. Zhao, D., Li, B., Xu, J., Hao, D., Jennings, N.R.: Selling multiple items via social networks. In: Proceedings of the 17th International Conference on Autonomous Agents and MultiAgent Systems, pp. 68–76 (2018). https://doi.org/10.5555/3237383.3237400

Incentives for Early Arrival in Cooperative Games: A Summary

Yaoxin Ge, Yao Zhang, and Dengji Zhao(✉)

ShanghaiTech University, Shanghai, China
{geyx,zhangyao1,zhaodj}@shanghaitech.edu.cn

Abstract. The present study concerns itself with the analysis of cooperative games in which players are required to join the game in a sequential manner. In such games, the value generated by those players who have joined at any given point must be irrevocably divided among the other players. Two criteria are proposed for the value division mechanism: firstly, that players should have incentives to join as early as possible, and secondly, that the division should be considered fair. In order to satisfy this requirement, it is necessary that each player's expected share in the mechanism should be equal to her Shapley value, assuming that the players' arrival order is uniformly random.

The primary technical contribution of this study is a comprehensive characterisation of 0-1 value games for which suitable mechanisms are available. We demonstrate that the Rewarding First Critical Player (RFC) mechanism is complete, in that a 0-1 value function admits a mechanism with the aforementioned properties if and only if RFC satisfies them. Furthermore, we provide an analytical characterisation of all such value functions.

Keywords: Cooperative Games · Early Arrival · Online Mechanisms

1 Introduction

Consider a frequent scenario, where a group of people form a partnership for a startup [Spender et al. (2017)]. They have different abilities or funds to contribute and can cooperate to create values. Sharing the value is a classic problem studied in the literature on cooperative games [Driessen (2013), Shapley (2016)]. Traditional cooperative games distribute the value after the whole coalition is formed. However, in reality, people typically do not all arrive at one point of time; rather, they join sequentially. This creates two issues: first, it is often not realistic to wait until everyone arrives before distributing the value—sometimes, it is not even clear if "everyone" has joined. This requires that values be distributed in an online manner. Second, the time to join can be strategic for a player; for example, a fund may choose the best time to invest in a startup.

In this work, we propose a theory for online cooperative games that explicitly addresses these issues. Firstly, we require that, after each player joins, an irrevocable distribution of the value created so far should be immediately determined.

We formalize a property called *online individually rational* to guarantee that players' shares be non-negative and non-decreasing as new players join, so that all are willing to participate till the end. Secondly, to gather resources quickly, and to prevent players from waiting indefinitely for each other to join first, we require a share-dividing mechanism to *incentivize players to join the game as early as possible*. Namely, we require the mechanism to distribute a higher reward to a player when she joins earlier (when the order of the others' arrivals remains fixed). We believe this is a critical property of an online value-sharing mechanism, which has not been discussed in the literature so far.

Incentivizing early arrival is the key property we proposed here, which also has promising applications. For example, considering a group of students working on a hard project which requires different combinations of skills to finish it, the supervisor may want to incentivize the students to join the project as early as possible so that the project can be finished earlier. Again for a startup to quickly get enough funds, they should design a proper reward sharing mechanism to incentivize investors to invest the startup as early as possible.

One may notice that there exist trivial online methods to incentivize early arrivals of players. For example, one may simply always give all the value to the first player in the game. However, such a solution is not fair (e.g., the first player may make no contribution to the value at all). Hence, we use the Shapley value [Shapley (2016)], a well-known and widely accepted classic solution to traditional cooperative game, as a benchmark for fairness [Clippel and Rozen (2019)]. More precisely, we require every player's expected reward over all possible joining orders to be exactly her Shapley value in the game, which is referred to as *Shapley-fair* in our setting.

Our main technical contribution is a complete characterization of 0-1 value games for which desired mechanisms exist. We show that a natural mechanism, Rewarding First Critical Player (RFC), is complete, in that a 0-1 value function admits a mechanism with the properties above if and only if RFC satisfies them; we analytically characterize all such value functions.

2 Related Work

Classic Cooperative Games

Investigation on classic cooperative games can be traced back to the last century [Roth (1988), Von Neumann and Morgenstern (2007)]. One of the main goals of these studies is to discuss which value distribution should be taken with a consideration of a set of axioms. This was initiated by Shapley value [Shapley (2016)], which is the foundation of almost all subsequent studies in [Young (1985)], the author characterized the monotone solutions in cooperative games along with Shapley value, and in [Hamiache (2001)], the author studied the associated consistency among series of games with identical Shapley value. More abundant investigations can be found in many surveys [Driessen (1991), Algaba et al. (2019)].

Different from the traditional research line, our work focuses on the setting where the players can strategically control the time of arrival to the cooperation. Therefore, our approach aligns more closely with a mechanism design standpoint, as we develop a method for distributing value that encourages arriving earlier.

Cooperative Games with Hierarchies

Many studies have already considered hierarchies or dynamics among players in cooperative games. For example, cooperative games were considered where only those coalitions of players are feasible that respect a given precedence structure (denoting the precedence of players' joining order) or permission structures (where players need others' permission to work) on the set of players in [Faigle and Kern (1992), Gilles et al. (1992)]. Moreover, generalized cooperative games, where different order of joining players bring different value, were considered in [Sanchez and Bergantinos (1997)], and [Zou et al. (2020)] considered this form and corresponding solutions to cooperative games with precedence structures.

The main difference of these studies from ours is that they treated the players' joining order or structural relationships as a constraint on the value function of the cooperative game, while in our work, a player's joining time is under her manipulation and we expect them to choose specific strategies (i.e., come as early as possible) by designing a proper online value distribution mechanism.

Mechanism Design in Dynamic Settings

Our approach has a similar perspective with the online mechanism design problem. For example, the auction mechanism design in dynamic environments, where players with private valuations of items will arrive or change over time was studied in [Pavan et al. (2014), Bergemann and Välimäki (2019), Parkes (2007)].

Another interesting trend of designing mechanisms with dynamic applications is diffusion incentives [Li et al. (2017), Zhao (2021), Li et al. (2022)]. They considered to incentivize the players to invite their neighbors in a social network to join an auction or a collaboration. Furthermore, online coalition formation is investigated in [FlamminiMichele et al. (2021), Bullinger and Romen (2023)]. The main objective of the study is to allocate the asynchronous joining players to groups in a way that maximizes the overall social welfare.

We consider a different setting for cooperative games, where players can control the time of arrival, and our goal of the mechanism design is to guarantee that they are benefited for early arrival. This has important applications to simulate swift collaborations.

3 The Model

An online cooperative game is given by a triple (N, v, π), where N is a set of players, $v : 2^N \to \mathbb{R}_+$ is a set function, and $\pi \in \Pi(N)$ is a permutation of N ($\Pi(N)$ denotes the set of all permutations of N). Players arrive sequentially, in the order given by π. A coalition is a set $S \subseteq N$ of players, who create a value $v(S)$. $v(\cdot)$ is *normalized* if $v(\emptyset) = 0$, and is *monotone* if $\forall T \subseteq S \subseteq N$, $v(S) \geq v(T)$. Throughout this work, we consider normalized and monotone games.

If a player i arrives earlier than j according to π, we say $i \prec_\pi j$. Let $p^\pi(i)$ denote the set of players that arrive (weakly) before i, including i: $p^\pi(i) := \{j \mid j \prec_\pi i\} \cup \{i\}$. For a subset $S \subseteq N$, v *restricted to* S, written as $v_{|S}$, is a set function $v_{|S} : 2^S \to \mathbb{R}_+$ defined as $v_{|S}(T) = v(T), \forall T \subseteq S$; π *restricted to* S, written as $\pi_{|S}$, is the permutation of S defined as $i \prec_{\pi_{|S}} j$ iff $i \prec_\pi j$, for all $i, j \in S$.

We look to divide the values in an online fashion as players join; that is, at any point of time, when the set of players that have arrived is S, we should allocate irrevocably to players in S all the value created by S, without the knowledge of v or π beyond the scope of S. We formalize this below.

Definition 1 (Prefix). *A coalition $S \subseteq N$ is a prefix of π if S is the set of first $|S|$ players to arrive according to π. This is denoted as $S \sqsubseteq \pi$.*

Definition 2 (Local Games). *For a game (N, v, π) and a prefix $S \sqsubseteq \pi$, the local game on S is the game $(S, v_{|S}, \pi_{|S})$.*

Definition 3. *A value-sharing policy ϕ maps a game (N, v, π) to an n-tuple of allocations, so that $\phi_i(N, v, \pi) \geq 0$ is player i's share of the value, and $\sum_i \phi_i(N, v, \pi) = v(N)$.*

An online value-sharing mechanism *is given by a value-sharing policy ϕ, so that after the arrival of each prefix $S \sqsubseteq \pi$, each player $i \in S$ gets a (cumulated) share of $\phi_i(S, v_{|S}, \pi_{|S})$.*

When the context is clear, we often omit the first argument of a policy ϕ, and simply write $\phi_i(v, \pi)$.

To keep the players from quitting early, we require each player's share to weakly increase as more players arrive:

Definition 4. *An online mechanism is* online individually rational *(OIR) for value function v if for any arrival order π and any $T, S \sqsubseteq \pi$ with $T \subseteq S$, we have $\phi_i(T, v_{|T}, \pi_{|T}) \leq \phi_i(S, v_{|S}, \pi_{|S})$ for every player $i \in T$.*

To prevent players from strategically delaying their arrivals, we require each player's share of value to be no larger if she chooses to join later than her actual arrival, assuming the other players' order of arrivals is fixed. Formally,

Definition 5. *An online mechanism is* incentivizing for early arrival *(I4EA) if for any player i, $\phi_i(N, v, \pi) \geq \phi_i(N, v, \pi')$ for all π and π' such that $\pi_{|N\setminus\{i\}} = \pi'_{|N\setminus\{i\}}$ and $p^\pi(i) \subsetneq p^{\pi'}(i)$.*

There are trivial mechanisms satisfying OIR and I4EA; consider, e.g., allocating, at any stage, all the current value to the first player. Such a mechanism, however, is easily seen to be unfair. One of the most celebrated notions for fairness in (offline) cooperative games is *Shapley value* (SV). Intuitively, the Shapley value for a player in an offline games is defined by a mental experiment involving an online game, where players arrive in an order that is uniformly at random; each player's expected *marginal contribution* in this mental experiment is then her Shapley value. Now for the truly online games that we study, it is natural to require that, in a mechanism considered fair, a player's expected share should equal her Shapley value if the arrival order is uniformly at random. We now formalize this discussion.

Definition 6 (Marginal Contribution). *Given a value function v, a player i's marginal contribution (MC) to a coalition $S \ni i$ is*

$$\mathrm{MC}(i, v, S) := v(S) - v(S \setminus \{i\}).$$

Definition 7 (Shapley Value, Shapley (2016)]). *Given a value function v, player i's Shapley Value (SV) is*

$$\mathrm{SV}_i(v) := \frac{1}{|N|!} \sum_{S \subseteq N \setminus \{i\}} |S|!(|N| - |S| - 1)!\,\mathrm{MC}(i, v, S \cup \{i\});$$

In a monotone game, the MC of any player in any coalition is non-negative; therefore, the SV is also non-negative.

Definition 8 (Shapley-Fair). *An online mechanism is Shapley-fair (SF) for a value function v if for each player $i \in N$,*

$$\frac{1}{|N|!} \sum_{\pi \in \Pi(N)} \phi_i(N, v, \pi) = \mathrm{SV}_i(v).$$

In this work, we aim to design online mechanisms that are OIR, I4EA and SF in games as broad as possible.

Two Simple Mechanisms

As a warm-up, we discuss two simple mechanisms. The first one computes the Shapley values for the local game on each prefix $S \sqsubseteq \pi$, and allocates these to the players in S. This mechanism is I4EA, because each player's eventual share is her Shapley value, regardless of the arrival order. However, this mechanism is not OIR as this SV may decrease (for example, in submodular games). The second simple mechanism awards each player, at her arrival, her MC to the existing coalition, and gives out no more share to this player in the future.

Definition 9. *In the* Distributing MC *(DMC) mechanism,*

$$\phi_i(v_{|S}, \pi_{|S}) = \mathrm{MC}(i, v, p^\pi(i)).$$

DMC is Shapley-fair by definition of SV. It is also easily seen to be OIR for monotone games. The following theorem shows that DMC is I4EA iff v is submodular.

Theorem 1. *DMC is I4EA if and only if the value function v is submodular.*[1]

4 0-1 Valued Monotone Games

In this section, we focus on valuation functions that take value only 0 or 1. Even for such simple functions, it is not a priori clear whether every function admits a mechanism that is OIR, I4EA and SF. A corollary of this section answers this question in the negative. The main technical contribution in this section is a mechanism, *Rewarding The First Critical Player* (RFC, Definition 11), which we show to be complete for 0-1 valuation functions, in the sense that for any 0-1 valued v that admits an OIR, I4EA and SF mechanism, RFC also satisfies these properties (Theorem 3). We also analytically characterize all such valuation functions (Theorem 4). We give a few examples in Sect. 4.3.

4.1 The RFC Mechanism

When v takes values only 0 or 1 and is monotone, for any arrival order π, there is at most one player whose arrival makes the current coalition's value jump from 0 to 1. We call this player the *marginal player* of (N, v, π). The RFC mechanism, in contrast, considers players that are indispensable in creating the positive value, and allocates the value to the first such player. Such indispensable players are called *critical*. Formally,

Definition 10. *Given a 0-1 valued v, for any S with $v(S) = 1$, define $S^* := \{j \in S \mid \mathrm{MC}(j, v, S) = 1\}$. For a 0-1 valued v and arrival order π, let i be the marginal player; the set of* critical players *is*

$$\mathrm{CR}(\pi, v) := (p^\pi(i))^*.$$

Recall that $p^\pi(i)$ is the coalition formed after i's arrival. In plain language, a player is critical if she is in $p^\pi(i)$ and if her removal makes the coalition's value drop to 0. By definition, the marginal player must be critical, but the set of critical players may include others. In the DMC mechanism, a critical player arriving earlier than the marginal player does not get allocated anything but may choose to delay her arrival to become the marginal player herself; this destroys incentive for early arrival. The RFC mechanism redresses this by awarding to the earliest among the critical players. Crucially, the set of critical players is fully determined by $v_{|p^\pi(i)}$ and $\pi_{|p^\pi(i)}$.

---

[1] A value function v is *submodular* if for every $S, T \subseteq N$ with $T \subseteq S$ and every $i \in N \setminus S$, we have $v(T \cup \{i\}) - v(T) \geq v(S \cup \{i\}) - v(S)$. v is *supermodular* if this inequality goes the other way for all such S, T and i.

Definition 11 (RFC). *The* Rewarding The First Critical Player *(RFC) mechanism is defined by the following value-sharing policy: for any prefix $S \sqsubseteq \pi$ with $v(S) = 1$, and player $i \in S$,*

$$\phi_i(v_{|S}, \pi_{|S}) = \begin{cases} 1, & \text{if } i \in \mathrm{CR}(\pi_{|S}, v_{|S}) \text{ and} \\ & \forall j \in \mathrm{CR}(\pi_{|S}, v_{|S}) \setminus \{i\}, i \preceq j, \\ 0, & \text{otherwise.} \end{cases}$$

For prefix S with $v(S) = 0$, no player gets allocated anything.

Theorem 2. *For all 0-1 valued, monotone v, RFC is OIR and SF.*

4.2 Completeness of RFC

The RFC mechanism was motivated to redress an incentive issue in the DMC mechanism. Perhaps surprisingly, we show that RFC not only outperforms DMC in the sense that it is I4EA for broader 0-1 valued games, but it is the best among all mechanisms for such valuation functions: whenever a 0-1 valued v admits an OIR, SF and I4EA mechanism, RFC is such a mechanism as well (Theorem 3). We then precisely characterize all such valuation functions(Theorem 4). Figure 1 illustrates the corresponding categorization of 0-1 valuation functions.

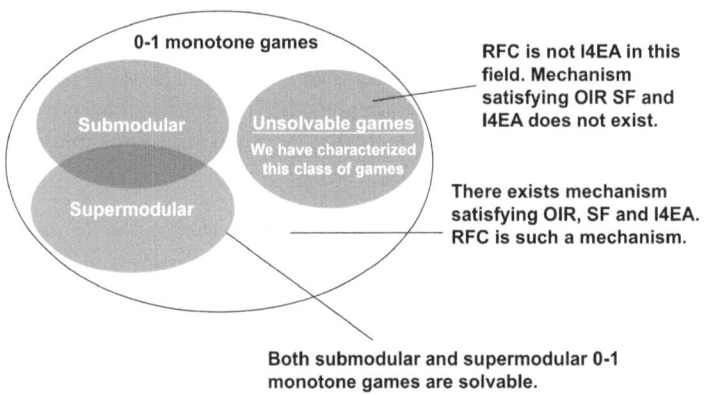

Fig. 1. Summary of the theorems mentioned in Sect. 4.2

Theorem 3. *For any 0-1 valued monotone v, if there exists a mechanism satisfying OIR, SF and I4EA, then RFC is such a mechanism.*

Theorem 4. *For any 0-1 valued monotone v, RFC is not I4EA if and only if there exists i such that $v(\{i\}) = 0$ and $\exists S, S^* = \{i\}$. (Recall the definition of S^* from Definition 10.)*

Corollary 1. *RFC is OIR, SF and I4EA on submodular and supermodular 0-1 valued monotone games.*

4.3 Examples

Example 1 shows a three-player valuation function that satisfies the condition in Theorem 4. We show in Proposition 1 that this is in fact the only three-player valuation with this property. We then give another valuation function in Example 2 that is neither submodular nor supermodular, for which RFC is OIR, SF and I4EA.

Example 1. Consider a game where $N = \{A, B, C\}$ and $v = [v(A), v(B), v(C), v(AB), v(AC), v(BC), v(ABC)] = [0, 0, 0, 0, 1, 1, 1]$, the marginal player and the critical players are listed in the 2nd column and 3rd column of Table 1. In the 4th column, we list the receivers of the values determined by RFC. In this game, RFC is not I4EA as we have $v(C) = 0$ and $\{A, B, C\}^* = \{C\}$. More specifically, in order $[A, C, B]$, C is the marginal player but not the unique critical player when she joins, so the value would be allocated to A. However, in order $[A, B, C]$, C is both the marginal player and the unique critical player when she joins, so she would get the value.

Table 1. The marginal player, critical players and the value receiver determined by RFC of game where $N = \{A, B, C\}$ and $v = [0, 0, 0, 0, 1, 1, 1]$ in every order.

Joining Order	Marginal Player	Critical Players	Value Receiver
[A,B,C]	C	C	C
[A,C,B]	C	A,C	A
[B,A,C]	C	C	C
[B,C,A]	C	B,C	B
[C,A,B]	A	C,A	C
[C,B,A]	B	C,B	C

Let $N = \{A, B, C\}$ and consider all possible 0-1 valued monotone games on N. Without loss of generality, we assume $v(C) \geq v(B) \geq v(A)$ and $v(BC) \geq v(AC) \geq v(AB)$. The games satisfying our assumption and the interpretations of the value allocations are listed in Table 2. $v = [0, 0, 0, 0, 1, 1, 1]$ is the only one that RFC is not I4EA.

Proposition 1. *For $N = \{A, B, C\}$ and v satisfying $v(C) \geq v(B) \geq v(A)$ and $v(BC) \geq v(AC) \geq v(AB)$, RFC is not I4EA if and only if $v = [0, 0, 0, 0, 1, 1, 1]$.*

Example 2. Consider a game where $N = \{A, B, C\}$ and $v = [0, 0, 0, 1, 1, 1, 1]$, notice that v is neither submodular nor supermodular as $v(AB) - v(B) = 1 > 0 = v(ABC) - v(BC) = v(A) - v(\emptyset)$. The RFC always allocates the value to the first joining player after the second player joins, which is I4EA.

Table 2. 3-player 0-1 valued monotone games and the interpretation of the value allocation on them.

v	Allocation of RFC	I4EA
[1,1,1,1,1,1]	To the first joining player	✓
[0,1,1,1,1,1]	To the first of $\{B, C\}$	✓
[0,0,1,1,1,1]	To C if she is the first or second. To first of $\{A, B\}$ in other case.	✓
[0,0,0,1,1,1]	To the first joining player	✓
[0,0,1,0,1,1]	To C.	✓
[0,0,0,0,1,1]	To C if she is the first or third. To first of $\{A, B\}$ in other case.	
[0,0,0,0,1,1]	To the first of $\{B, C\}$	✓
[0,0,0,0,0,1]	To the first joining player	✓

5 Future Work

There are several future directions worth investigation. For 0-1 valued monotone games, one may consider to characterize a whole set of mechanisms satisfying all the properties on solvable games. For general monotone games, the characterization of all solvable games is still open and there might exist other decomposition that works on more games. It is also worth studying the I4EA property in offline (make the decisions until everyone joined) or other (such as cost-sharing and hedonic game) settings.

Acknowledgements. This work is supported by Science and Technology Commission of Shanghai Municipality (No. 22ZR1442200 and No. 23010503000), and Shanghai Frontiers Science Center of Human-centered Artificial Intelligence (ShangHAI).

Disclosure of Interests. The authors have no competing interests to declare that are relevant to the content of this article.

References

Algaba, E., Fragnelli, V., Sánchez-Soriano, J.: Handbook of the Shapley Value. CRC Press, Boca Raton (2019)

Bergemann, D., Välimäki, J.: Dynamic mechanism design: an introduction. J. Econ. Lit. **57**(2), 235–274 (2019)

Bullinger, M., Romen, R.: Online coalition formation under random arrival or coalition dissolution. In: Gørtz, I.L., Farach-Colton, M., Puglisi, S.J., Herman, G. (eds.) 31st Annual European Symposium on Algorithms, ESA 2023, 4–6 September 2023, Amsterdam, The Netherlands. LIPIcs, vol. 274. Schloss Dagstuhl - Leibniz-Zentrum für Informatik, pp. 27:1–27:18 (2023)

De Clippel, G., Rozen, K.: Fairness through the lens of cooperative game theory: an experimental approach. SSRN Electron. J. (2019)

Driessen, T.S.H.: A survey of consistency properties in cooperative game theory. SIAM Rev. **33**(1), 43–59 (1991)

Driessen, T.S.H.: Cooperative Games, Solutions and Applications, vol. 3. Springer, Heidelberg (2013)

Faigle, U., Kern, W.: The Shapley value for cooperative games under precedence constraints. Internat. J. Game Theory **21**(1992), 249–266 (1992)

Flammini, M., Monaco, G., Moscardelli, L., Shalom, M., Zaks, S.: On the online coalition structure generation problem. J. Artif. Intell. Res. (2021)

Gilles, R.P., Owen, G., van den Brink, R.: Games with permission structures: the conjunctive approach. Int. J. Game Theory **20**(3), 277–293 (1992)

Hamiache, G.: Associated consistency and Shapley value. Internat. J. Game Theory **30**(2001), 279–289 (2001)

Li, B., Hao, D., Gao, H., Zhao, D.: Diffusion auction design. Artif. Intell. **303**, 103631 (2022)

Li, B., Hao, D., Zhao, D., Zhou, T.: Mechanism design in social networks. In: Proceedings of the AAAI Conference on Artificial Intelligence, vol. 31 (2017)

Parkes, D.C.: Online mechanisms. In: Algorithmic Game Theory, pp. 411–439 (2007)

Pavan, A., Segal, I., Toikka, J.: Dynamic mechanism design: a myersonian approach. Econometrica **82**(2), 601–653 (2014)

Roth, A.E.: The Shapley value: essays in honor of Lloyd S. Shapley. Cambridge University Press, Cambridge (1988)

Sanchez, E., Bergantinos, G.: On values for generalized characteristic functions. Operations-Research-Spektrum **19**(3), 229–234 (1997)

Shapley, L.S.: A value for n-person games. In: Contributions to the Theory of Games (AM-28), Volume II, pp. 307–318. Princeton University Press (2016)

Spender, J.-C., Corvello, V., Grimaldi, M., Rippa, P.: Startups and open innovation: a review of the literature. Eur. J. Innov. Manag. **20**(1), 4–30 (2017)

Von Neumann, J., Morgenstern, O.: Theory of games and economic behavior (60th Anniversary Commemorative Edition). Princeton University Press (2007)

Young, H.P.: Monotonic solutions of cooperative games. Int. J. Game Theory **14**(2), 65–72 (1985)

Zhao, D.: Mechanism design powered by social interactions. In: Dignum, F., Lomuscio, A., Endriss, U., Nowé, A. (eds.) AAMAS 2021: 20th International Conference on Autonomous Agents and Multiagent Systems, Virtual Event, United Kingdom, 3–7 May 2021, pp. 63–67. ACM (2021). https://www.ifaamas.org/Proceedings/aamas2021/pdfs/p63.pdf

Zou, Z., Zhang, Q., Borkotokey, S., Yu, X.: The extended Shapley value for generalized cooperative games under precedence constraints. Oper. Res. **20**, 899–925 (2020)

A Strategy-Proof and Collusion-Proof Peer Grading Mechanism

Bin Li[✉] and Xiaoyu Du

Nanjing University of Science and Technology, Nanjing, China
{cs.libin,duxy}@njust.edu.cn

Abstract. The practice of grading candidates according to their performance is widespread and of utmost importance, where the key is to assess each candidate's performance with reliable information. This paper aims to investigate peer grading in scenarios with ground truths, where there is an unknown ground truth represented by a real number for each candidate's performance. The final grade assigned to each candidate is determined by the assessments, which are assumed as unbiased estimators of the candidate's ground truth, made by both the experts and the candidates. We are interested in peer grading mechanisms that not only provide unbiased grades but are also resistant to strategic behaviors such as unilateral strategy deviation and collusion, which poses a challenging task in peer mechanism design. Generally, we make two contributions to the study of peer grading. First, we establish the impossibility of designing non-trivial grading mechanisms when the number of candidates is less than three. Second, we propose a practical and non-trivial grading mechanism, called the mean externality mechanism, for settings with at least three candidates, which is proved to be unbiased, strategy-proof and collusion-proof.

Keywords: Peer grading · Strategy-Proofness · Collusion-Proofness

1 Introduction

Grading candidates according to their performance is a universal problem, occurring when recruiting, admitting students, reviewing scientific papers, and more [2]. Providing reliable grades is crucial to assess the quality of candidates, which could even make an influential impact on the career of candidates in certain fields [20]. Often, the performance of candidates is judged by a number of experts, while in some scenarios there may be a lack of qualified experts to perform an effective assessment. A typical example is grading students in "massive open online courses", or simply MOOCs. The massive student participation makes it impossible (or extremely costly) to provide reliable assessments for all students. In addition, evaluating a large number of students by few teachers is likely to be both tedious and cognitively demanding. To alleviate the problem, many peer grading mechanisms have been proposed [3,5,6,13], in which candidates, like students, performers or employees, are asked to grade the performance of their peers. Peer mechanisms have a variety of high-stakes applications, including grading in a course [19], deciding aids targeted to people in need [1,7], giving loans to entrepreneurs [12], etc. As candidates' reports may impact their final grades, manipulation becomes a real problem in peer mechanism design, where candidates can take opportunities to manipulate the outcomes in their favor. Evidences of strategic behaviors have been found in employee promotion [11], art competition [4], academic peer review [8, 14], etc., and ensuring a fair and impartial grading process cannot be over emphasized [17].

There are generally two kinds of strategic behaviors in peer mechanisms. The most common one is unilateral strategy deviation, where an individual candidate may influence her grade by misreporting her evaluations on the peers. One technique to prevent such kind of manipulation is to partition candidates into groups [3, 9, 10], in which each candidate can only influence the grade of a peer outside of her group. For example, the mechanism designer can divide candidates into several groups and candidates in one group only grade the candidates of other groups. In addition, one candidate can also be part of different groups. In the permutation mechanism [9], the candidates are placed in random order and the mechanism only counts nominations from peers that are before the current candidate in the order. As each candidate can only impact if a peer wins when the candidate is no longer able to win, misreporting in the permutation mechanism is not beneficial. Besides partitioning the candidates, another approach is to enlarge the set of possible winners such that the candidates who could win via strategic reports are also included [13, 18].

Another issue occurring in peer mechanisms is collusion: the candidates can collude if they can communicate. A typical case appears in academic peer review, where one researcher gives another researcher a positive review on their paper in exchange for a positive review in return [8, 14]. Previous results show that preventing all forms of collusion seems impossible. In the model of nominating candidates for a fixed number of winners [3], the authors proved the impossibility of designing a group-strategy-proof peer mechanism with any finite approximation ratio. Even if we cannot design peer mechanisms immune to collusion, the challenge of discouraging and detecting collusion is still important [15]. In another work on poverty targeting [16], the author showed that collusion can be alleviated by limiting the aid budget. Besides these early attempts, we know little about how to prevent or discourage collusion in peer mechanisms.

In this paper, we focus our attention on peer grading in scenarios where ground truths are present. Specifically, we assume that there is an unknown ground truth, which is represented by a real number, for each candidate's performance. The final grade of the candidate is determined by the assessments, which are unbiased estimators of the candidate's ground truth, given by both experts and peers. Given the above setting, we are interested in designing peer grading mechanisms immune to both unilateral deviation and collusion, which presents a changeling task in peer mechanism design. We prove that when the number of candidates is less than three, then only trivial grading mechanisms can be both strategy-proof and collusion-proof. For the scenario with at least three candidates, we propose a novel non-trivial grading mechanism, called the mean externality mechanism, which satisfies strategy-proofness, collusion-proofness and other desirable properties. To evaluate the performance of the proposed mechanism, we further conduct extensive experiments using synthetic data. The experimental results demonstrate the superiority of our mechanism in achieving lower grade loss.

The remainder of the paper is organized as follows. We first define the problem of peer grading with ground truths and some related concepts in Sect. 2. Then, in Sect. 3 we introduce a basic grading mechanism that does not consider the manipulation issue. Following the weak performance of the basic grading mechanism in strategic environments, we propose our mean externality mechanism and analyze its properties in Sect. 4.

2 Preliminaries

Consider a peer grading setting where there is a set C of candidates and a set E of experts. For each candidate $i \in C$, we assume there is a ground truth $\mu_i \in \mathcal{R}_+$ which represents the correct or "true" assessment of candidate i' performance quality. We model the assessment of an individual $i \in C \cup E$ on candidate $j \in C$ as a random variable with the cumulative distribution $F_{i,j}$ with a mean of μ_j and support $[\underline{s}, \overline{s}]$. Formally, given any two candidates $i, j \in C$, we use s_i^j, which is sampled from $F_{i,j}$, to denote the score of candidate i on the performance of candidate j. For convenience, let $\mathbf{s}_i^r = (s_i^j)_{j \in C}$ denote the scores of all candidates given by i, and $\mathbf{s}_i^c = (s_j^i)_{j \in C}$ denote the scores given to i by all candidates. In addition, denote by s the score profile given by all candidates, i.e., $\mathbf{s} = (s_i^j)_{i,j \in C} = (\mathbf{s}_i^r)_{i \in C} = (\mathbf{s}_i^c)_{i \in C}$. Besides peer assessments s, we use b_i^j, which is sampled according to $F_{i,j}$, to represent candidate j' score assessed by expert i. Similarly, let $\mathbf{b}_i^r = (b_i^j)_{j \in C}$ and $\mathbf{b}_i^c = (b_j^i)_{j \in E}$ denote the scores of all candidates given by expert i and the scores given to candidate i by all experts, respectively. Denote by b the score profile given by all experts, i.e., $\mathbf{b} = (b_i^j)_{i \in E, j \in C} = (\mathbf{b}_i^r)_{i \in E} = (\mathbf{b}_i^c)_{i \in C}$. Based on the score profiles of the candidates and experts, a grading mechanism, which is defined below, will determine the final grades of all candidates.

Definition 1. *A grading mechanism $\mathcal{G}$ is defined by a set of grading functions $\{g_i : \mathcal{S} \times \mathcal{B} \to \mathcal{R}\}_{i \in C}$, where g_i is the grading function for candidate i, and $\mathcal{S}$ and $\mathcal{B}$ denote the spaces of the score profiles of the candidates and experts, respectively.*

Let s denote the true score profile of all candidates and $\tilde{\mathbf{s}}$ denote the reported score profile. For convenience's sake, let x_{-i} denote the remaining set of x that excludes i's report e.g., $\tilde{\mathbf{s}}_{-i} = \tilde{\mathbf{s}} \setminus \tilde{\mathbf{s}}_i^r$ represents the reported scores of all candidates without i. In our model, the experts are treated as neutral agents, i.e., they always report true assessments on the candidates' performance. Next, we define several desirable properties that a practical grading mechanism should satisfy.

Definition 2. *A grading mechanism $\mathcal{G}$ is non-trivial (NT) if the following two conditions are satisfied:*

- **Non-Expert-Dictatorship (NED):** *for all b and all candidates $i \in C$, there exist at least two score profiles s and s' such that $g_i(\mathbf{s}, \mathbf{b}) \neq g_i(\mathbf{s}', \mathbf{b})$.*
- **Non-Candidate-Dictatorship (NCD):** *for all s and all candidates $i \in C$, there exist at least two score profiles b and b' such that $g_i(\mathbf{s}, \mathbf{b}) \neq g_i(\mathbf{s}, \mathbf{b}')$.*

Definition 3 (Strategy-Proofness). *A grading mechanism $\mathcal{G}$ is strategy-proof (SP) if*

$$g_i(\mathbf{s}_i^r, \tilde{\mathbf{s}}_{-i}^r, \mathbf{b}) \geq g_i(\tilde{\mathbf{s}}_i^r, \tilde{\mathbf{s}}_{-i}^r, \mathbf{b}) \tag{1}$$

for all $i \in C$, all $\mathbf{s}_i^r$, all $\tilde{\mathbf{s}}_i$ and all $\mathbf{b}$.

Definition 4 (Collusion-Proofness). *A grading mechanism $\mathcal{G}$ is collusion-proof (CF) if for all $i \in C$, all $\mathbf{s}$ and all $\mathbf{b}$, there exists no other score profile $\tilde{\mathbf{s}}$ such that*

$$g_i(\tilde{\mathbf{s}}, \mathbf{b}) \geq g_i(\mathbf{s}, \mathbf{b}), \tag{2}$$

and the inequality strictly holds for at least one candidate.

Definition 5 (Consistency). *A grading mechanism $\mathcal{G}$ is consistent (CI) if*

$$\mathbb{E}[g_i(\mathbf{s}, \mathbf{b})] = \mu_i, \tag{3}$$

where the expectation is take over all realizations of $(\mathbf{s}, \mathbf{b})$.

3 The Basic Grading Mechanism

In this section, we introduce a basic grading mechanism and analyze its properties. In the mechanism, teachers provide an overall evaluation on all students' performance and students grade each other.

The Basic Grading Mechanism (BGM)

Given reported score profiles $\tilde{\mathbf{s}}$ and $\mathbf{b}$, i's final grade $g_i(\tilde{\mathbf{s}}, \mathbf{b})$ is defined as

$$m(\mathbf{b}) + m(\tilde{\mathbf{s}}_i^c) - m(\tilde{\mathbf{s}}), \tag{4}$$

where $m(X) = \frac{\sum_{j \in X} x_j}{|X|}$ denotes the sample mean.

In the BGM, each candidate's final grade is divided into two components: $m(\mathbf{b})$ and $m(\tilde{\mathbf{s}}_i^c) - m(\tilde{\mathbf{s}})$. The former component $m(\mathbf{b})$ is the average score of all candidates graded by all experts, which reflects the average performance of all candidates from an expert perspective. The latter $m(\tilde{\mathbf{s}}_i^c) - m(\tilde{\mathbf{s}})$ indicates the difference between candidate i's performance and the average from a candidate perspective. Intuitively, the BGM converts the assessments of all experts into a base score and characterizes individual differences by all candidates' assessments[1]. Figure 1 presents a running example of the BGM with three candidates and two experts. We next analyze the properties of the BGM.

---

[1] Though the experts are asked to report their assessments on all candidates, in practice it is sufficient for each expert to provide an assessment on the average performance of all candidates.

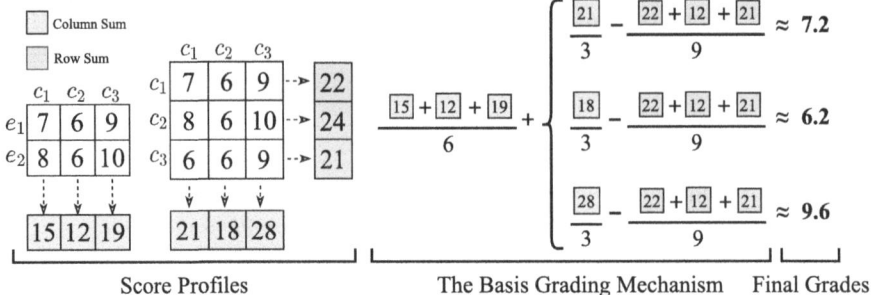

Fig. 1. A running example of the BGM when all candidates submit their true scores.

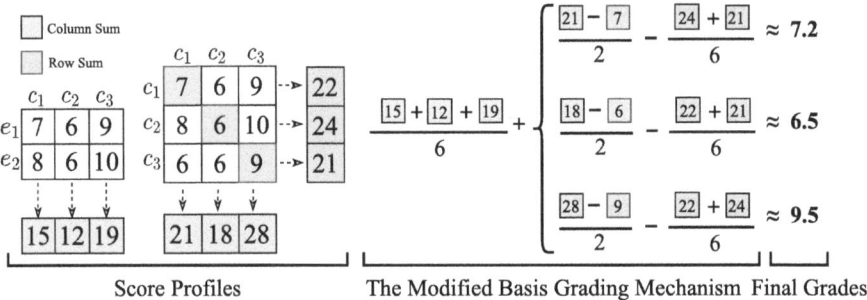

Fig. 2. A running example of the MBGM.

Proposition 1. *Suppose all candidates act truthfully, then the BGM is NT and CI*[2].

The BGM is a good choice for the grading mechanism when all candidates act truthfully. However, we next show that in the BGM candidates can take opportunities to manipulate the outcomes in their favor, i.e., the BGM is not SP.

Lemma 1. *In the BGM, the following strategy is a dominant strategy for $i \in C$:*

$$s_i^j = \begin{cases} \overline{s} & j = i, \\ \underline{s} & j \neq i. \end{cases}$$

Proposition 2. *Suppose all candidates act strategically, then the BGM is a trivial grading mechanism.*

Recall that in the BGM, candidate i's report $\tilde{s}_i^r$ takes part in her own grade, this is the reason why the BGM is not SP. To resolve the manipulation issue, we can eliminate i's self assessment in her grading function g_i. Lemma 2 shows that this is the only way to prevent unilateral strategy deviation.

Lemma 2. *A grading mechanism $\mathcal{G}$ is strategy-proof if and only if for all candidates i and all reported score profile $(\tilde{\mathbf{s}}, \mathbf{b})$, $g_i(\tilde{\mathbf{s}}, \mathbf{b})$ is independent of i's report $\tilde{s}_i^r$.*

---
[2] The missing proofs are deferred to the full version.

For example, we can modify the basic grading mechanism by eliminating all self assessments in each candidate's grading function. Now, in the modified basic grading mechanism (short for MBGM), candidate i's grade is given by

$$m(\mathbf{b}) + m(\tilde{\mathbf{s}}_i^c \setminus s_i^i) - m(\tilde{\mathbf{s}} \setminus \mathbf{s}_i^r). \tag{5}$$

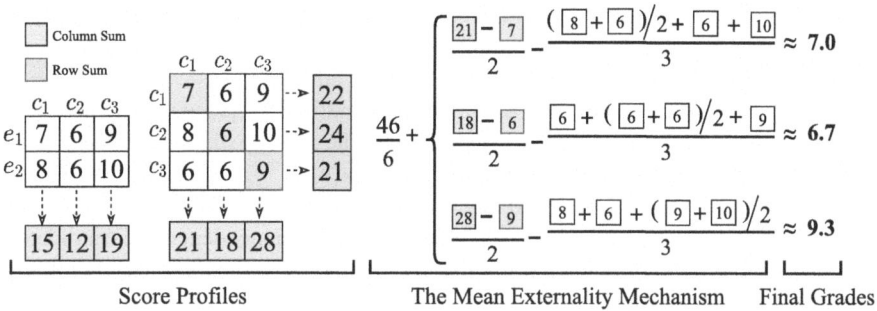

Fig. 3. A running example of the MEM.

We can easily verify that the MBGM is NT, SP and CI. Figure 2 demonstrates a running example of the MBGM. Though the MBGM owns many nice properties, the candidates can collude together to increase their final grades, i.e., it is not CP. Considering the score profiles presented in Fig. 1 and the following strategy: For any candidate i, set her self assessment by $\tilde{s}_i^i = 0$ and all other candidates j's score by $\tilde{s}_i^j = 10$. If all candidates follow the above strategy, then all the three candidates can increase their final grades to 11 in the MBGM. A natural question arises: Is there any grading mechanism which satisfies all the desirable properties, including NT, SP, CT and CI. Our next result demonstrates that there is no non-trivial grading mechanism that satisfies SP and CP in settings with fewer than three candidates.

Theorem 1. *Suppose $|C| < 3$, then no non-trivial grading mechanism is SP and CP.*

In the next section we propose a novel grading mechanism in settings with at least three candidates which fulfills all the desirable properties.

4 The Mean Externality Mechanism

In this section, we propose a novel grading mechanism, called the mean externality mechanism (short for MEM) for settings with at least three candidates. Technically speaking, the MEM is a variant of the BGM and is formally defined below.

The Mean Externality Mechanism (MEM)

Given reported score profiles $\tilde{\mathbf{s}}$ and $\mathbf{b}$, i's final grade $g_i(\tilde{\mathbf{s}}, \mathbf{b})$ is defined as

$$m(\mathbf{b}) + m(\tilde{\mathbf{s}}_i^c \setminus s_i^i) - m(\{m(\tilde{\mathbf{s}}_j^c \setminus \{s_j^j, s_i^j\})\}_{j \in C}). \tag{6}$$

Intuitively, the MEM can be built from the BGM through the following three steps: For each candidates $i \in C$, we first eliminate all i's assessments, which ensures the property of strategy-proofness. Then, we eliminate all candidates' self assessments. Given the updated score profile $\tilde{\mathbf{s}} \setminus \{\mathbf{s}_i^r, \{s_j^j\}_{j \in C}\}$, finally we replace the original average performance of all candidates, namely $m(\tilde{\mathbf{s}})$, by the average of all candidates' average scores in the updated score profile, that is $m(m(\mathbf{s}_1^{c,new}), s, m(\mathbf{s}_{|C|}^{c,new}))$. The last two steps guarantee that the proposed mechanism is unbiased and also immune to candidates' collusion. As the final grade of each candidate is independent of all candidates' self assessments, we refer to the new grading mechanism as the mean externality mechanism. Figure 3 demonstrates a running example of the MEM. Before presenting our main result, we first give two lemmas.

Lemma 3. *In the MEM, the equation $\sum_{i \in C} g_i(\tilde{\mathbf{s}}, \mathbf{b}) = |C| \cdot m(\mathbf{b})$ holds for all reported score profiles $\tilde{\mathbf{s}}$ and $\mathbf{b}$.*

For example, the sum of the three candidates' final grades given in Fig. 3 is 23 which is identical to $|C| \cdot m(b) = 3 \cdot \frac{46}{6}$.

Lemma 4. *Given any set of score profiles $\{\mathbf{s}^i\}_{i \in C}$ where $\mathbf{s}^i \subseteq \mathbf{s}_i^c$ is non-empty for all $i \in C$, we have that*

$$\mathbb{E}[m(\{m(\mathbf{s}^i)\}_{i \in C})] = \frac{\sum_{i \in C} \mu_i}{|C|}. \tag{7}$$

Based on Lemmas 3 and 4, we show MEM satisfies all the desirable properties.

Theorem 2. *Suppose $|C| \geq 3$, then the MEM is NT, SP, CP and CI.*

To handle the scenario of a large number of candidates, we next propose a scalable MEM by partitioning participants into small-scale groups.

The (p, q)-Mean Externality Mechanism ((p, q)-MEM)

Given a set E of experts and a set C of candidates, the (p, q)-MEM is defined as follows:

- **Partitioning:** Divide E into p disjoint groups, denoted by $E_1, E_2, \cdots, E_p$, and C into q disjoint groups, denoted by $C_1, C_2, \cdots, C_q$.

- **Matching:** Predefine a matching function $f : \{1, \cdots, q\} \to \{1, \cdots, p\}$, where given a group of candidates C_z, $E_{f(z)}$ represents the expert group assigned to C_z.
- **Grading:** For each participant group $(C_z, E_{f(z)})$, let $\tilde{\mathbf{s}}^{C_z} = \{s_i^j\}_{i,j \in C_z}$ and $\mathbf{b}^{E_f(z)} = \{b_i^j\}_{i \in E_{f(z)}, j \in C_z}$ be the score profiles reported in the group. Then, the final grade of candidate $i \in C_z$ is defined by $g_i^{mem}(\tilde{\mathbf{s}}^{C_z}, \mathbf{b}^{E_{f(z)}})$.

The following result is straightforward based on Theorem 2.

Corollary 1. *Suppose $|C_z| \geq 3$ and $|E_{f(z)}| \geq 1$ for all $z = 1, \cdots, q$, then the (p, q)-MEM is NT, SP, CP and CI.*

5 Conclusion

In this paper, we investigate how to design peer grading mechanisms that are resistant to strategic behaviors of the peers. In settings where the number of candidates is less than three, we prove that there exists no non-trivial peer grading mechanism that is both strategy-proof and collusion-proof. Then, we turn to the scenarios with at least three candidates, and propose a novel peer grading mechanism which is proved to be strategy-proof and collusion-proof. In order to reduce the amount of reported assessments, we further introduce a scalable MEM by partitioning the participants into groups.

Acknowledgments. We thank Yanyan Zhang for helpful discussions. This work was supported by the National Natural Science Foundation of China No. 62202229.

References

1. Alatas, V., Banerjee, A., Hanna, R., Olken, B.A., Purnamasari, R., Wai-Poi, M.: Self-targeting: evidence from a field experiment in Indonesia. J. Polit. Econ. **124**(2), 371–427 (2016)
2. de Alfaro, L., Shavlovsky, M.: Crowdgrader: a tool for crowdsourcing the evaluation of homework assignments. In: Proceedings of the 45th ACM Technical Symposium on Computer Science Education, pp. 415–420 (2014)
3. Alon, N., Fischer, F., Procaccia, A., Tennenholtz, M.: Sum of us: strategyproof selection from the selectors. In: Proceedings of the 13th Conference on Theoretical Aspects of Rationality and Knowledge, pp. 101–110 (2011)
4. Balietti, S., Goldstone, R.L., Helbing, D.: Peer review and competition in the art exhibition game. Proc. Natl. Acad. Sci. **113**(30), 8414–8419 (2016)
5. Caragiannis, I., Krimpas, G.A., Panteli, M., Voudouris, A.A.: Co-rank: an online tool for collectively deciding efficient rankings among peers. In: Proceedings of the Thirtieth AAAI Conference on Artificial Intelligence, pp. 4351–4352 (2016)
6. Caragiannis, I., Krimpas, G.A., Voudouris, A.A.: Aggregating partial rankings with applications to peer grading in massive online open courses. In: Proceedings of the 2015 International Conference on Autonomous Agents and Multiagent Systems, pp. 675–683 (2015)

7. Conning, J., Kevane, M.: Community-based targeting mechanisms for social safety nets: a critical review. World Dev. **30**(3), 375–394 (2002)
8. Ferguson, C., Marcus, A., Oransky, I.: Publishing: the peer-review scam. Nature **515**, 480–482 (2014)
9. Fischer, F., Klimm, M.: Optimal impartial selection. In: Proceedings of the Fifteenth ACM Conference on Economics and Computation, pp. 803–820 (2014)
10. Holzman, R., Moulin, H.: Impartial nominations for a prize. Econometrica **81**(1), 173–196 (2013)
11. Huang, Y., Shum, M., Wu, X., Xiao, J.Z.: Discovery of bias and strategic behavior in crowd-sourced performance assessment (2019)
12. Hussam, R., Rigol, N., Roth, B.N.: Targeting high ability entrepreneurs using community information: mechanism design in the field. Am. Econ. Rev. **112**(3), 861–98 (2022)
13. Kurokawa, D., Lev, O., Morgenstern, J., Procaccia, A.D.: Impartial peer review. In: Proceedings of the 24th International Conference on Artificial Intelligence, pp. 582–588 (2015)
14. Littman, M.L.: Collusion rings threaten the integrity of computer science research. Commun. ACM **64**(6), 43–44 (2021)
15. Olckers, M., Walsh, T.: Manipulation and peer mechanisms: a survey (2022)
16. Rai, A.S.: Targeting the poor using community information. J. Dev. Econ. **69**(1), 71–83 (2002)
17. Shah, N.B., Tabibian, B., Muandet, K., Guyon, I., Von Luxburg, U.: Design and analysis of the nips 2016 review process. J. Mach. Learn. Res. **19**(1), 1913–1946 (2018)
18. Tamura, S., Ohseto, S.: Impartial nomination correspondences. Soc. Choice Welfare **431**, 47–54 (2014)
19. Topping, K.: Peer assessment between students in colleges and universities. Rev. Educ. Res. **68**(3), 249–76 (1998)
20. Xu, Y., Zhao, H., Shi, X.: Mechanism design for paper review. Retrieved from Carnegie Mellon University, School of Computer Science (2017). https://www.cs.cmu.edu/~nihars/teaching/10709-Fa17/Fa17projects/mechanismReview.pdf

A Summary of Distributed Mechanism Design in Social Networks

Haoxin Liu[✉] and Yao Zhang

ShanghaiTech University, Shanghai, China
{liuhx,zhangyao1}@shanghaitech.edu.cn

Abstract. The latest trend in auction design involves creating mechanisms that encourage buyers to bring new participants into the auction through their social networks [18]. This presents a unique challenge because buyers are in competition with each other, and effective incentives must be crafted to motivate them to invite peers. Various intriguing mechanisms have been developed for single-item sales, but they all depend on the trustworthiness of the seller or a third party to ensure proper implementation. Additionally, these mechanisms may compromise privacy by exposing the connections of participants. To address these issues, distributed mechanisms that protect privacy are more desirable in practice. In this paper, we introduce the first distributed auction mechanism in social networks that maintains the confidentiality of buyers' connections and achieves full decentralization without relying on a trustworthy intermediary. Furthermore, our mechanism's centralized reduction presents an interesting approach to calculating participants' contributions, offering a distinct improvement over existing methods.

Keywords: Distributed mechanism design · Invitation incentive · Social network

1 Introduction

Recent research in AI has increasingly focused on mechanism design within social networks [9,18]. This approach leverages participants' connections to enhance engagement by encouraging them to invite additional participants, thereby expanding the reach of the mechanism. However, the competitive nature among participants presents a challenge, necessitating the development of new mechanisms to attract a larger audience. Some significant progress has been made in areas such as auctions, matching, and coalitional games [6,8,16].

In this paper, we extend the investigation into network-based auctions for item sales. Traditional mechanisms in this area are centralized, relying on the seller or a trustworthy third party to oversee and execute the process. This central authority, however, gains access to all participants' private connections, raising concerns about privacy. To address this, our objective is to design a distributed auction system for networks that operates without a central authority and safeguards participants' privacy by keeping their connections confidential.

In contrast to centralized systems, which concentrate the execution within a single authority, distributed mechanisms spread this responsibility across all participants. This shift requires participants to engage in additional activities beyond merely submitting their private information, thus expanding their range of actions and complicating efforts to prevent manipulative behavior.

In this context, we introduce an innovative distributed mechanism for selling a single item within a network that operates independently of any trusted overseer. Our approach also presents a fresh method for incentivizing participants to recruit others. Specifically, each participant's reward is determined by their effectiveness in linking the seller with the final buyer and their success in attracting other high-value buyers.

1.1 Related Work

Auctions in Social Networks. In social networks, the pioneering auction method designed to motivate users to invite their connections is known as the Information Diffusion Mechanism (IDM) [10]. IDM operates by rewarding the critical nodes to the highest bid. Zhao and his team [18] expanded this concept to accommodate auctions involving multiple identical items, with each participant needing just one item. Later, Li and colleagues [9] identified the essential conditions required to ensure incentive compatibility in single-item auctions within social networks. A detailed overview of related research can be found in [6].

Invitation Incentives in Other Contexts. The concept of encouraging participant recruitment by invitations extends beyond social networks to various game-theoretic scenarios. Kawasaki et al. [8] and Cho et al. [1] developed strategies to motivate invitations in matching markets, while Zhang et al. [16] proposed a model for invitation incentives within cooperative games. Zhao [17,18] provides a comprehensive review of these approaches across different contexts.

Distributed Mechanism Design. The field of distributed mechanism design has been extensively explored. Monderer and Tennenholtz [11] pioneered research on a basic single-item distributed auction problem where agents must relay messages to a central authority. Feigenbaum et al. [2,3] introduced the concept of distributed algorithmic mechanism design. Parkes and Shneidman [12] and Petcu et al. [13] examined the distributed execution of the VCG mechanism, offering principles for computational distribution. Additionally, Shneidman and Parkes [14] investigated distributed implementations in interdomain routing. Our study draws from the formal specifications for distributed mechanism design detailed in [15] and highlights other relevant contributions in [4,5].

Unlike distributed mechanisms that depend on third parties, our approach achieves full decentralization without the need for any trustworthy intermediary.

2 The Model

We consider a scenario where a seller, denoted as S, is selling a single item within a social network. We represent the network as an undirected graph $G = (V, E)$, where $V = N \cup \{S\}$ denotes the set of all nodes, and the edge set E includes all connections between these nodes. The set $N = \{1, 2, \ldots, n\}$ comprises all potential buyers, each with a private valuation $v_i \geq 0$ for receiving the item and a set of neighbors $r_i \subseteq V \setminus \{i\}$, where $j \in r_i$ if there is an edge between i and j in E. Specifically, r_S denotes the set of neighbors of the seller. We assume that communication is only direct between neighboring nodes, reflecting a feature of modern social networks. Formally, let $\theta_i = (v_i, r_i)$ represent the private **type** of buyer $i \in N$, and $\Theta_i = \mathbb{R}_{\geq 0} \times \mathcal{P}(V)$ denote the type space of i, where $\mathcal{P}(V)$ is the power set of V. The joint vector $\theta = (\theta_1, \theta_2, \ldots, \theta_n)$ represents the type profile of all buyers, and $\Theta = \Theta_1 \times \Theta_2 \times \cdots \times \Theta_n$ denotes the type profile space. We define θ_{-i} as the type profile of all buyers except i, and θ can be expressed as (θ_i, θ_{-i}). We first provide some definitions for centralized mechanisms. We say a mechanism M is *incentive compatible* if truthfully revealing one's type is a dominant strategy for a buyer, regardless of the reports of other buyers.

Definition 1. *A centralized mechanism $M = (\pi, p)$ is **incentive compatible** (IC) if for all $i \in N$, all $\theta_i' \in \Theta_i$ and all $\theta_{-i}' \in \Theta_{-i}$,*

$$u_i(\theta_i, (\theta_i, \theta_{-i}'), (\pi, p)) \geq u_i(\theta_i, (\theta_i', \theta_{-i}'), (\pi, p)).$$

Another desirable property ensures that a buyer will not incur a loss in the mechanism as long as she truthfully reports her type.

Definition 2. *A centralized mechanism $M = (\pi, p)$ is **individually rational** (IR) if for all buyers $i \in N$, all $\theta_i \subseteq \Theta_i$, and $\theta_{-i}' \in \Theta_{-i}$,*

$$u_i(\theta_i, (\theta_i, \theta_{-i}'), (\pi, p)) \geq 0.$$

As a result, ensuring that buyers follow the mechanism correctly becomes crucial in distributed settings. To address this, we introduce the concept of *strategy* to describe a buyer's behavior across all states of the mechanism. Let s_i represent the strategy of buyer i, which is parameterized by i's type θ_i, and let Σ_i denote i's strategy space, encompassing all possible strategies available to i. A strategy profile is defined as $s(\theta) = (s_1(\theta_1), s_2(\theta_2), \ldots, s_n(\theta_n))$, where θ represents the type profile of all buyers, and $s_{-i}(\theta) = (s_j(\theta_j))_{j \neq i, j \in N}$ denotes the strategies of all buyers other than i.

Definition 3. *A distributed mechanism d^M is a 3-tuple $d^M = (\Sigma, (\pi, p), s^M)$, where $\Sigma = (\Sigma_1, \ldots, \Sigma_n)$ is the strategy space of all buyers, $\pi = \{\pi_i\}_{i \in N}$ is the allocation function, $p = \{p_i\}_{i \in N}$ is the payment function, and $s^M = (s_1^M, \ldots, s_n^M) \in \Sigma$ is the intended strategy of the mechanism. Particularly, $\pi_i : \Sigma \to \{0, 1\}$ and $p_i : \Sigma \to \mathbb{R}$ are the allocation and payment functions for i respectively.*

For each buyer i, the intended strategy $s_i^M \in \Sigma_i$ can be viewed as a series of algorithms or actions prescribed by the mechanism for buyer i to follow. This strategy s_i^M is dependent on buyer i's private type θ_i, with $s_i^M(\theta_i)$ specifying the actions that buyer i should undertake in each state of the mechanism. In a decentralized setting, however, the strategy space is highly complex and lacks a standard structure, encompassing a variety of actions beyond just reporting the type. To address this, we refer to the canonical literature [15] and decompose the strategy s_i into three distinct types of actions: $s_i = (t_i, q_i, f_i)$, where t_i represents the information-revelation action, q_i denotes the message-passing action, and f_i corresponds to the computational action. Similarly, the intended strategy s_i^M can also be expressed as (t_i^M, q_i^M, f_i^M).

We must now update the notation to $\pi(s(\theta))$ and $p(s(\theta))$, reflecting the sequence of actions taken by the buyers. Consequently, the utility for a buyer is revised to $u_i(\theta_i, s(\theta), (\pi, p)) = \pi_i(s(\theta)) \cdot v_i - p_i(s(\theta))$. In this context, achieving incentive compatibility (IC) may be challenging, as there might not be a single computational strategy that is optimal regardless of the actions of other buyers [4]. Therefore, we will consider a more practical solution concept known as *ex-post incentive compatibility*, which represents a feasible approach to distributing computation among buyers.

Definition 4. *A distributed mechanism $d^M = (\Sigma, (\pi, p), s^M)$ is **ex-post incentive compatible** if for all $\theta \in \Theta$, all buyers $i \in N$, and all $s_i \in \Sigma_i$, $u_i(\theta_i, (s_i^M, s_{-i}^M), (\pi, p)) \geq u_i(\theta_i, (s_i, s_{-i}^M), (\pi, p))$.*

This implies that no participant can achieve a higher utility by deviating from the equilibrium where all individuals follow their prescribed strategies. If a mechanism is ex-post incentive compatible (IC), then the strategy profile s^M constitutes an ex-post Nash equilibrium.

Additionally, for any buyer $i \in N$, if her strategy is restricted to $s_i(\theta_i) = (t_i, q_i^M, f_i^M)$, there always exists a centralized mechanism M such that the expected outcome $E[\pi(s(\theta'))]$ matches the outcome $\pi'(\theta')$ of the centralized mechanism, and the expected payment $E[p(s(\theta'))]$ aligns with the payment $p'(\theta')$ of the centralized mechanism. Here, π represents the outcome of the distributed mechanism d^M, and π' denotes the outcome of the corresponding centralized mechanism M, while p and p' are the payment functions for these mechanisms, respectively. This centralized mechanism M is referred to as the *centralized reduction mechanism* (CRM) of d^M, and we say that d^M constitutes a *distributed implementation* of M.

3 The Mechanism

In this part, we provide a formal explanation of the initial distributed mechanism in social networks named as the *Sequential Resale Auction* (SRA).

3.1 Sequential Resale Auction

We outline the distributed auction as a process consisting of three stages, with buyers engaging in various activities during each one. In the initial stage, buyers share sale information with their neighbors. During the second stage, they gather bids from their invited neighbors and present these bids to participate in the sale. In the final stage, sequential resales occur from the seller to the ultimate winner.

Stage 1 (Top-down Diffusion): The first stage is *top-down diffusion*, during which the sale information is disseminated through the social network starting from the original seller S. Each recipient of the information can determine her bid v'_i and selectively invite neighbors r'_i from her set of neighbors based on her own preferences. When buyer i invites a neighbor $j \in r'_i$ to participate in the sale, the edge e_{ij} represents a directed edge from i to j, making buyer i an *inviter* of buyer j. However, buyer i should avoid re-inviting her own inviters, as she recognizes that these individuals have already been informed of the sale from her perspective, thus no further invitations are needed. The combined actions of deciding on a bid and choosing which neighbors to invite form the buyer's information-revelation action for this stage, which is formally defined as follows.

Definition 5 (Information-revelation Action). *Given buyer i's type $\theta_i = (v_i, r_i)$, her information-revelation action t_i is to decide her bid v'_i in the sale and choose neighbors $r'_i \subseteq \tilde{r}_i$ to invite, i.e., $t_i = (v'_i, r'_i)$. The intended information-revelation action is to truthfully reveal her type, i.e., $t_i^M = (v_i, \tilde{r}_i)$.*

The information-revelation action in this context is analogous to the reporting action found in centralized mechanisms. However, unlike centralized scenarios where a buyer reports both her valuation and her neighbors to the seller, in this decentralized setting, a buyer only needs to invite her own chosen neighbors and is not required to disclose her valuation to anyone. The diffusion of information continues until it reaches buyers who have only their inviters as neighbors. These buyers, having an out-degree of zero in the graph structure, can be considered as the leaf nodes of the network. Ultimately, the social network evolves into a connected directed graph G' that includes all valid buyers. It is important to note that this graph remains unknown to any individual buyer, who is only aware of who invites her and whom she invites.

Stage 2 (Bottom-up Aggregation): The second stage is *bottom-up aggregation*. This stage begins with the leaf nodes, which are required to transmit their bids v'_i to their inviters, thus participating in the preceding auction. An intermediate buyer, upon receiving bids from invited neighbors, must aggregate these into a new bid termed the *aggregated bid* and pass it to her own inviters recursively. This process involves the buyer's computational action f_i and message-passing action q_i. For simplicity, let $b_i \in \mathbb{R}_{\geq 0}$ denote the aggregated bid of buyer i, and let B_i represent the set of all bids received from her invited neighbors. The computational action f_i corresponds to an aggregation algorithm that combines B_i and the buyer's own bid v'_i into a new bid b_i. We denote the set of all possible aggregation algorithms as F.

Definition 6 (Computational Action). *Given buyer i's bids set B_i, and her bid v'_i, the computational action $f_i \in F$ will generate aggregated bid $b_i = f_i(B_i, v'_i)$. The intended computational action f_i^M is to select the largest among the bids she is aware of as her aggregated bid, i.e., $f_i^M(B_i, v'_i) = \max(B_i \cup \{v'_i\})$.*

After generating the aggregated bid b_i, the next decision for a buyer is to determine whether to report b_i accurately and select which inviters to send the message to. Misreporting b_i as b'_i can be viewed as using an alternative aggregation method that yields the misreported value b'_i and reporting b'_i truthfully. This form of manipulation is thus categorized as a computational action, and it is assumed that buyers will report their aggregated bids honestly when considering the message-passing action. Consequently, the message-passing action is concerned solely with the reporting of the aggregated bid to one or more inviters. We represent the set of all possible message-passing actions by buyers as Q.

Definition 7 (Message-passing Action). *Buyer i's message-passing action $q_i \in Q$ is to select a subset from her inviters set arbitrarily to report her aggregated bid, i.e., $q_i \in \mathcal{P}(r_i^{inv})$. The intended message-passing action is to randomly select only one inviter, i.e., $q_i^M \sim Uniform(r_i^{inv})$, where $Uniform(\cdot)$ indicates the uniform distribution.*

For an inviter who receives the aggregated bid from buyer i, the actual origin of the bid remains unknown, thereby safeguarding the privacy of buyers' valuations. The second stage concludes once the original seller has collected all the aggregated bids from her neighbors. Provided that all buyers carry out the specified message-passing actions, the social network will transform into a directed tree, as each buyer designates a single other buyer as their parent node.

Stage 3 (Top-down Allocation): The third stage involves *top-down allocation*, where the auction is conceptualized as a series of subsequent sales, each termed a *local auction*. If the item is currently resold to buyer i, she has the authority to start a local auction and extend invitations to all her Stage 1 neighbors to join, including those who did not relay messages to her during Stage 2. If buyer j is eligible for this local auction but did not transfer her bid to i in Stage 2, there must be a direct link between i and j, and j must have chosen a different inviter to collect her bid in the earlier stage. To ensure fairness and prevent other buyers from using j's bid against her, j should only connect to the current seller i and sever connections with all prior inviters. Those affected by this disconnection must recalculate and re-aggregate their bids. The following outlines the definition of a local auction conducted by buyer i:

Definition 8 (Local Auction). *A local auction hosted by buyer i, $\hat{M}_i$, is composed of a local allocation function $\hat{\pi}^i = \{\hat{\pi}_j^i\}_{j \in r'_i}$ and a local payment function $\hat{p}^i = \{\hat{p}_j^i\}_{j \in r'_i}$, where $\hat{\pi}_j^i \in \{0,1\}$ and $\hat{p}_j^i \in \mathbb{R}$ are the local allocation and local payment for participant j respectively.*

Seller i computes the local allocation outcome $\hat{\pi}^i$ and the corresponding payment outcome $\hat{p}^i$ based on the set of bids she has received, B_i, her own bid v'_i, and the price she previously paid to acquire the item, $\bar{p}_i$. This price acts as the reserve price in a standard VCG auction. The process of local auctions continues iteratively starting from the seller, until one participant decides to retain the item. These iterative auctions create a resale sequence.

Sequential Resale Auction (SRA)

(1) **Top-down diffusion.** The initial seller S begins by sharing the auction information with her adjacent nodes. Upon learning of the auction, each informed buyer performs her action of revealing information, denoted by $t_i = (v'_i, r'_i)$. This action includes her bid v'_i and the subset of neighbors $r'_i \subseteq \tilde{r}_i$ that she chooses to invite. As a result, the social network evolves into a directed graph G'.

(2) **Bottom-up aggregation.** Each buyer performs the message-passing action q_i to convey the outcome of their computational action $b_i = f_i(B_i, v'_i)$ to their inviters. This phase begins with all leaf nodes and continues until the original seller has received the aggregated bids from all of her neighbors.

(3) **Top-down allocation.** The initial local auction is started by the seller S. In a local auction hosted by i, let $b^{1st}_{r'_i}$ and $b^{2nd}_{r'_i}$ represent the highest and second-highest bids among all participants, respectively. The local allocation and payment functions for a participant $j \in r'_i$ are defined as follows:

- **Local allocation function:**

$$\hat{\pi}^i_j = \begin{cases} 1, & \text{if } v'_j = b^{1st}_{r'_i}, \text{ and } v_i < \max\{\bar{p}_i, b^{2nd}_{r'_i}\}, \\ 0, & \text{otherwise.} \end{cases} \quad (1)$$

- **Local payment function:**

$$\hat{p}^i_j = \begin{cases} \max\{\bar{p}_i, b^{2nd}_{r'_i}\}, & \text{if } \hat{\pi}^i_j = 1, \\ 0, & \text{otherwise.} \end{cases} \quad (2)$$

Upon the completion of the local auction $\hat{M}_i$, the local winner w (i.e., $\hat{\pi}^i_w = 1$) will conduct the subsequent local auction $\hat{M}_w$. The payment made by w in $\hat{M}_i$ will become the purchasing price $\bar{p}_w$ for the new local auction $\hat{M}_w$. The entire resale process concludes if a local seller i retains the item, which occurs if $\Sigma_{j \in r'_i} \hat{\pi}^i_j = 0$.

3.2 Centralized Reduction of the SRA

In a centralized setting, all participants adhere to the prescribed message-passing and computational procedures, with each individual having control solely over the disclosure of their private type in their information-revelation stage, represented by $t_i = (v'_i, r'_i)$. Under this setting, the seller can efficiently identify the highest bidder, denoted as z, where $v'_z = v^{1st}_{G(\theta')}$ and $v^{1st}_{\mathcal{D}} = \max_{i \in \mathcal{D}} v'_i$ represents the highest reported valuation within the subset $\mathcal{D} \subseteq G(\theta')$.

In the centralized reduction mechanism, a spanning tree T is randomly generated from $G(\theta')$, following the second stage of our distributed auction where the social network transitions into a randomized tree. Let $\mathcal{T}$ denote the set of all potential spanning trees. The seller can then identify the simple path from S to z within each spanning tree. We define a specific category of paths and demonstrate how it relates to the resale path in the third stage of our distributed auction.

Definition 9. A ***diffusion path*** *to buyer m is a simple path from S to m, represented as $h^m = (h_0, h_1, \ldots, h_k)$, where $h_0 = S$, $h_k = m$, and it fulfills the condition that for any two buyers h_i and h_j ($i < j - 1$), there are no edges connecting h_i and h_j in the graph $G(\theta')$. In other words, a diffusion path does not contain any back-edges between its buyers.*

For every spanning tree, if the path from S to z is not classified as a diffusion path, we apply a modification to the path. The modification process is as follows: for each back-edge that exists between vertices h_i and h_j (where $i < j - 1$) along the path h^z, remove all intermediate nodes between h_i and h_j on this path and insert the back-edge directly into the path. This modification corresponds to the operation discussed previously.

Centralized Reduction Mechanism of the SRA

---

(1) Given a reported type profile $\theta' \in \Theta$, construct the subgraph $G(\theta')$ consisting of all valid buyers. Next, identify the valid buyer z within $G(\theta')$ who has the maximum valuation, using random tie-breaking if needed.
(2) For a spanning tree T generated from $G(\theta')$, check if the simple path from S to z is a diffusion path. If it is, go to (4); otherwise, go to (3).
(3) Transform the simple path to a diffusion path.
(4) Let the diffusion path from S to z be denoted by $h^z = \{S, h_1, h_2, \ldots, z\}$. Define T_{-i} as the subset of buyers in the tree excluding the buyer i. Allocate the item within the current spanning tree using an allocation function that can be defined recursively as follows:

$$\pi_i^T(\theta') = \begin{cases} 1 \text{ if } i = h_j \in h^z, v_i' = v_{T_{-h_{j+1}}}^{1st}, \\ \quad \text{and } \sum_{k \in T_{-i}} \pi_k^T(\theta') = 0, \\ 0 \text{ otherwise.} \end{cases} \quad (3)$$

(5) Denote the winner as $w = h_l \in h^z$. The payment function for the current spanning tree is defined as:

$$p_i^T(\theta') = \begin{cases} v_{T_{-w}}^{1st} & \text{if } i = w, \\ v_{T_{-h_j}}^{1st} - v_{T_{-h_{j+1}}}^{1st} & \text{if } i = h_j \in h^z, j < l, \\ 0 & \text{otherwise.} \end{cases} \quad (4)$$

(6) For every potential spanning tree derived from $G(\theta')$, repeat steps (2) through (5). During this process, for each buyer $i \in G(\theta')$, record the total number of wins as $cnt(i)$ and the total payments as $sum(p_i^T)$.

> (7) Denote the number of all possible spanning trees as $|\mathcal{T}|$. The overall allocation function and payment function are defined as:
>
> $$\pi_i(\theta') = \frac{cnt(i)}{|\mathcal{T}|}, \quad p_i(\theta') = \frac{sum(p_i^T)}{|\mathcal{T}|} \qquad (5)$$

3.3 Generalization in Multi-item Problems of the SRA

The Sequential Resale Auction is the first distributed diffusion auction mechanism in social networks achieving full decentralization, and the idea about distributed resale is worthy of further exploration. We will describe the extension of this mechanism in the context of multi-item auction problems in this section.

We will firstly extend the diffusion auction model described before to accommodate the challenges posed by multi-item diffusion auctions within social networks. In order to simulate the real process of selling items within social networks, we assume any user in the social network can potentially act as a seller. And we begin our attempts by focusing on the homogeneous multi-item auction problem, in which the seller can sell an identical set of $K(K \geq 1)$ items. In this paper, we adhere to the problem setting used in classic homogeneous multi-item auction mechanisms such as the Generalized Information Diffusion Mechanism (GIDM), modeling buyers' valuations for identical items as a single-value function. Specifically, each buyer $i \in N$ possesses a constant valuation for the items on sale [7,19]. Therefore, under this setting, a buyer's private type is still her valuation v_i on the item and her neighbor set r_i, i.e., $\theta_i = (v_i, r_i)$. All other settings remain unchanged, which also applies in the distributed settings. However, differing from GIDM and similar mechanisms that typically assume each buyer requires at most one item, we relax this constraint and therefore buyers can demand an unlimited number of items up to the maximum available quantity of K. But we still assume that a buyer's valuation function does not diminish marginally with an increase in the number of items she wins.

In this setting, the SRA mechanism described previously can be naturally extended to accommodate the homogeneous multi-item problem, where the original seller can execute K rounds of sequential resale auctions in order to allocate these items in a decentralized manner. Since each buyer randomly selects an invitee in the second stage of the sequential resale auction mechanism, the mechanism is a stochastic mechanism, with each execution potentially producing different outcomes as illustrated in Fig. 1. However, it ensures that the allocation and payment results from each outcome satisfy the ex-post incentive compatibility property (as proven in Theorem 2), thus we can consider each execution as a distinct allocation process for one of the homogeneous items awaiting sale. Even the whole sale ends up with the same buyer receiving all items, the resale paths of the items during each round of auction may differ due to the potential variation in the aggregated graphs generated after the second stage of the mechanism. This means that the buyers who participate in the resale process and thereby gained utilities may also vary across runs. This reveals the significance and value of repeatedly executing this mechanism for K rounds.

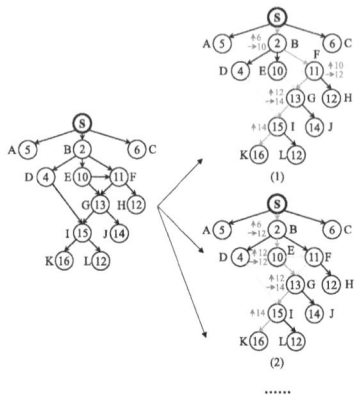

Fig. 1. The social network may produce different allocation and payment results.

Extension to the SRA for homogeneous multi-item auction

1. A seller in the social network decides to sell K identical items, she can conduct the top-down diffusion stage to spread the auction information among the social network, and form the diffusion graph G'.
2. Conduct K rounds of sequential resale auction, in each round, conduct:
   (a) Execute the bottom-up aggregation stage and form the diffusion graph G^{agg}.
   (b) Execute the top-down allocation stage on the formed diffusion graph, local sellers make transactions and pass the item, until some buyer chooses to keep the item.
   (c) Record the transaction information on the distributed ledger, then the round of auction ends, and repeat a new round of auction.
3. Repeat K rounds of auctions, until all items are sold.

---

4 Evaluations

In this section, we offer a theoretical analysis of the sequential resale auction (SRA) and perform simulation experiments to evaluate how it compares to traditional centralized mechanisms, including the Information Diffusion Mechanism, which represents existing centralized approaches. Initially, we demonstrate that when all buyers follow the intended strategy, the amount a buyer pays does not depend on their bid.

Lemma 1. *When all participants conduct the intended message-passing and computational actions, the payment of each buyer is independent of her bid.*

We further demonstrate that, in the SRA, no buyer will experience negative utility as long as they bid their true valuation and all participants carry out the intended message-passing and computational actions.

Theorem 1. *The SRA is individually rational.*

We now prove that the intended strategy s^M forms an ex-post Nash equilibrium for all participants. In other words, no individual buyer can improve their utility by unilaterally deviating from the proposed strategy.

Theorem 2. *The SRA is ex-post incentive compatible.*

In distributed mechanism design, it is typical to achieve ex-post incentive compatibility (IC), but strict IC is rarely feasible. This is because when one agent deviates, others may adjust their actions to counterbalance the deviation. In contrast, the centralized Sequential Resale Auction (SRA) preserves IC, as its execution is governed by a central authority. Each randomly selected resale path operates in a manner similar to the Information Diffusion Mechanism (IDM), which has been shown to satisfy IC in [10].

Furthermore, our mechanism guarantees the seller's revenue will not be lower than that obtained through the traditional VCG mechanism applied among only neighbors. This assurance enhances the appeal of our mechanism for sellers.

Experiments Based on Simple Networks. Additionally, we conducted simulation experiments to compare our proposed mechanism with other centralized methods. For this comparison, we selected the Information Diffusion Mechanism [10], which is one of the earliest mechanisms in social networks.

Our experiment is performed on the network depicted in Fig. 2. Each buyer's valuation distribution depends on their distance from the seller. Specifically, buyers located farther from the seller are more likely to have higher valuations. This setup helps to illustrate the features of diffusion auctions, as the objective is to identify higher bids within the network. We sample 10^4 instances based on the specified distributions and apply both the SRA and IDM to these instances. Notably, since the SRA is a randomized mechanism, we compute the average over 10^3 runs to estimate the expected outcome. We record the winning probabilities and average utilities for both mechanisms across all 10^4 samples.

The results of the experiment are summarized in Figs. 3(a) and 3(b). Figure 3(a) illustrates the distribution of winning probabilities for all buyers, while Fig. 3(b) displays the expected utilities for each buyer. From these findings, we observe that our mechanism provides more equitable winning opportunities

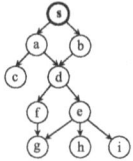

Fig. 2. The network for the experiment.

for all participants. Additionally, it offers rewards to a greater number of buyers, particularly benefiting those located near the seller and non-critical buyers (e.g., buyers a and b), who receive minimal rewards under the IDM. This approach encourages buyers close to the seller and those less critical to be more inclined to participate in the diffusion process. Therefore, our mechanism is distinguished by its complete decentralization and ability to operate without the need for a trusted central authority, which constitutes our main contribution.

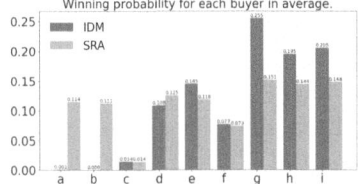

(a) Winning probability for each buyer in average.

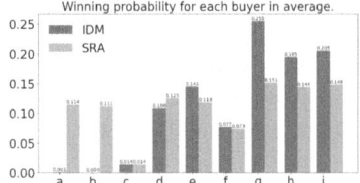

(b) Utility for each buyer in average.

Fig. 3. Experiment results for each buyer in average.

Experiments Based on Complex Networks. In addition to experiments conducted on a representative network structure, we employ three different methodologies to randomly generate various types of networks and carry out more generalized simulation experiments on these complex network configurations. The types of networks we examine include *small-world networks*, *scale-free networks*, and *random networks*. Our experiments aim to highlight the significant contribution of our mechanism: achieving a fairer reward distribution. We will measure the number of buyers who receive positive utilities as an indicator to compare different mechanisms in this context.

The three types of networks are generated randomly, guided by three parameters: the total number of nodes in the network, the average number of connections per node, and the likelihood of an edge being created between any two nodes. We categorize all experiments into three groups based on the three types of network structures. Within each group, we configure the networks to have scales of 15, 30, 45, and 60 nodes, while maintaining a fixed average degree of either 3 or 4 neighbors per node. For each sample of these network structures, we perform 100 iterations of user valuation sampling for the item, calculating the number of buyers who achieve positive utilities across the two mechanisms for each iteration. The average of these iterations serves as the final result (Figs. 4 and 6).

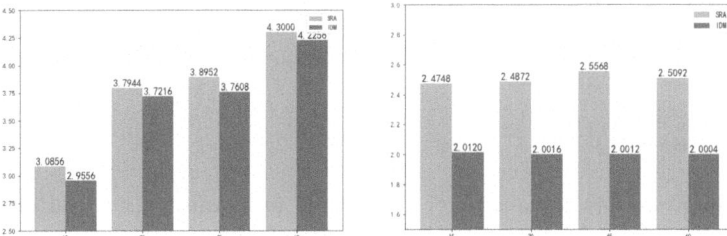

Fig. 4. Average number of nodes with positive utilities in small-world networks.

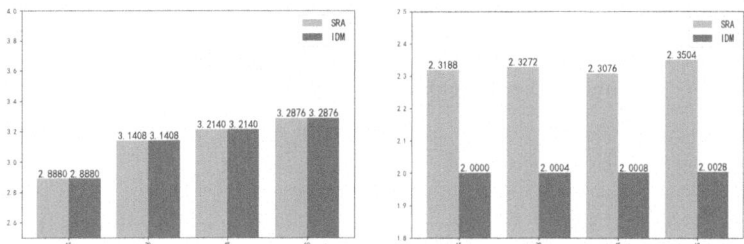

Fig. 5. Average number of nodes with positive utilities in scale-free networks.

These figures illustrate the comparative results. In each set of comparison figures, the left sub-figures display the outcomes when the average number of neighbors is set to 3, while the right sub-figures present results for an average of 4 neighbors. It is clear from all the charts that the SRA achieves a higher average number of nodes obtaining positive utilities compared to the IDM. Notably, in the case of scale-free networks with an average of 3 neighbors, which is essentially a tree structure, the experimental results from both mechanisms are nearly identical, as shown in Fig. 5. The Sequential Resale Auction mechanism does not depend on specific nodes, such as cut-points. Instead, it promotes resale and reward distribution through complete diffusion paths, allowing more participants to receive rewards and encouraging active engagement with the mechanism. Furthermore, since real-world social networks typically exhibit this high degree of connectivity, the Sequential Resale Auction mechanism holds considerable practical relevance in real-world scenarios.

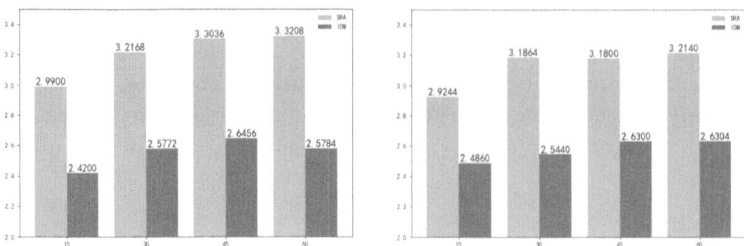

Fig. 6. Average number of nodes with positive utilities in random networks.

5 Conclusion

In this paper, we introduce a novel distributed mechanism for social networks, termed the Sequential Resale Auction. This mechanism offers full decentralization and operates independently of any reliable third parties. Additionally, we describe a centralized reduction method for our distributed auction, highlighting its unique benefits. This approach not only facilitates rewarding a broader range of participants, including those who are not crucial to the auction process, but also enhances the overall effectiveness of the mechanism.

Disclosure-of-Interest Statement. The authors have no competing interests to declare that are relevant to the content of this article.

References

1. Cho, S., Todo, T., Yokoo, M.: Two-sided matching over social networks. In: Raedt, L.D. (ed.) Proceedings of the Thirty-First International Joint Conference on Artificial Intelligence, IJCAI 2022, Vienna, Austria, 23–29 July 2022, pp. 186–193. ijcai.org (2022)
2. Feigenbaum, J., Papadimitriou, C.H., Sami, R., Shenker, S.: A BGP-based mechanism for lowest-cost routing. In: Proceedings of the Twenty-First Annual ACM Symposium on Principles of Distributed Computing, PODC 2002, Monterey, California, USA, 21–24 July 2002, pp. 173–182. ACM (2002)
3. Feigenbaum, J., Papadimitriou, C.H., Shenker, S.: Sharing the cost of multicast transmissions. J. Comput. Syst. Sci. **63**(1), 21–41 (2001)
4. Feigenbaum, J., Schapira, M., Shenker, S.: Distributed algorithmic mechanism design. In: Algorithmic Game Theory, vol. 14, pp. 363–384. Cambridge University Press, Cambridge (2007)
5. Feigenbaum, J., Shenker, S.: Distributed algorithmic mechanism design: recent results and future directions. In: Proceedings of the 6th International Workshop on Discrete Algorithms and Methods for Mobile Computing and Communications (DIAL-M 2002), pp. 1–13. ACM (2002)
6. Guo, Y., Hao, D.: Emerging methods of auction design in social networks. In: Zhou, Z. (ed.) Proceedings of the Thirtieth International Joint Conference on Artificial Intelligence, IJCAI 2021, Virtual Event/Montreal, Canada, 19–27 August 2021, pp. 4434–4441. IJCAI (2021)

7. Kawasaki, T., Barrot, N., Takanashi, S., Todo, T., Yokoo, M.: Strategy-proof and non-wasteful multi-unit auction via social network. In: Proceedings of the AAAI Conference on Artificial Intelligence, vol. 34, pp. 2062–2069 (2020)
8. Kawasaki, T., Wada, R., Todo, T., Yokoo, M.: Mechanism design for housing markets over social networks. In: Proceedings of the 20th International Conference on Autonomous Agents and Multiagent Systems, pp. 692–700 (2021)
9. Li, B., Hao, D., Gao, H., Zhao, D.: Diffusion auction design. Artif. Intell. **303**, 103631 (2022)
10. Li, B., Hao, D., Zhao, D., Zhou, T.: Mechanism design in social networks. In: Thirty-First AAAI Conference on Artificial Intelligence, pp. 586–592. AAAI Press (2017)
11. Monderer, D., Tennenholtz, M.: Distributed games: from mechanisms to protocols. In: Proceedings of the Sixteenth National Conference on Artificial Intelligence and Eleventh Conference on Innovative Applications of Artificial Intelligence, 18–22 July 1999, Orlando, Florida, USA, pp. 32–37. AAAI Press/The MIT Press (1999)
12. Parkes, D.C., Shneidman, J.: Distributed implementations of vickrey-clarke-groves mechanisms. In: Proceedings of the Third International Joint Conference on Autonomous Agents and Multiagent Systems, AAMAS 2004, pp. 261–268 (2004)
13. Petcu, A., Faltings, B., Parkes, D.C.: Mdpop: faithful distributed implementation of efficient social choice problems. In: Proceedings of the International Joint Conference on Autonomous Agents and Multi Agent Systems (AAMAS 2006), pp. 1397–1404 (2006)
14. Shneidman, J., Parkes, D.C.: Using redundancy to improve robustness of distributed mechanism implementations. In: Proceedings 4th ACM Conference on Electronic Commerce (EC-2003), San Diego, California, USA, 9–12 June 2003 (2003)
15. Shneidman, J., Parkes, D.C.: Specification faithfulness in networks with rational nodes. In: Proceedings of the Twenty-Third Annual ACM Symposium on Principles of Distributed Computing, pp. 88–97 (2004)
16. Zhang, Y., Zhao, D.: Incentives to invite others to form larger coalitions. In: 21st International Conference on Autonomous Agents and Multiagent Systems, AAMAS 2022, Auckland, New Zealand, 9–13 May 2022, pp. 1509–1517. International Foundation for Autonomous Agents and Multiagent Systems (IFAAMAS) (2022)
17. Zhao, D.: Mechanism design powered by social interactions. In: 20th International Conference on Autonomous Agents and Multiagent Systems, AAMAS 2021, pp. 63–67. ACM (2021)
18. Zhao, D.: Mechanism design powered by social interactions: a call to arms. In: Proceedings of the Thirty-First International Joint Conference on Artificial Intelligence, IJCAI 2022, pp. 5831–5835 (2022)
19. Zhao, D., Li, B., Xu, J., Hao, D., Jennings, N.R.: Selling multiple items via social networks. In: Proceedings of the 17th International Conference on Autonomous Agents and MultiAgent Systems, pp. 68–76. International Foundation for Autonomous Agents and Multiagent Systems, Richland, SC (2018)

Author Index

A
Ågotnes, Thomas 36

C
Christoff, Zoé 36

D
Du, Xiaoyu 86

G
Ge, Xu 1
Ge, Yaoxin 76

H
Hadfi, Rafik 52
Hao, Dong 65

I
Ito, Takayuki 52

L
Li, Bin 1, 65, 86
Liu, Haoxin 95
Liu, Yuchen 52

M
Matsushita, Akira 19

Z
Zhang, Yao 76, 95
Zhao, Dengji 1, 76
Zheng, Junjie 1

SPRINGER NATURE

GPSR Compliance

The European Union's (EU) General Product Safety Regulation (GPSR) is a set of rules that requires consumer products to be safe and our obligations to ensure this.

If you have any concerns about our products, you can contact us on ProductSafety@springernature.com

In case Publisher is established outside the EU, the EU authorized representative is:

Springer Nature Customer Service Center GmbH
Europaplatz 3
69115 Heidelberg, Germany

The manufacturer's authorised representative in the EU is Springer Nature Customer Service Centre GmbH, Europaplatz 3, 69115 Heidelberg, Germany. If you have any concerns regarding our products, please contact ProductSafety@springernature.com

Printed and bound by CPI Group (UK) Ltd, Croydon, CR0 4YY

26/03/2026

02078952-0017